ABANDON FOOLISH SCHEME

ABANDON FOOLISH SCHEME

Deathly encounters that you won't
find in bestsellers about dying

JOHN FRY

Book design by Tina Christensen
Cover artwork by Leslie Fry

ISBN: 978-0-578-23506-6 (paperback)
ISBN: 978-0-578-23507-3 (ebook)

ALSO BY JOHN FRY

A Mind at Sea

The Story of Modern Skiing

No Hill Too Fast

CONTENTS

CHAPTER 16

IN MEMORIAM 130

My experiences at memorial services and funerals, and how to make these a radiant experience, not a stultifying, incoherent event. How to write a winning obituary.

CHAPTER 17

AN ODDITY OF GRIEF 140

To mourn a death in the deepest, most trenchant way raises ironic, if not profound, questions about what it means to grieve. How much worse I suffer from the death of my dog than that of a human friend or relative.

CHAPTER 18

LIFE AFTER DEATH? 146

I address the inevitable question—outgrowths of my published work on Sir Arnold Lunn. Scientists warm to the idea that consciousness has an independent existence to which we connect in varied ways.

CHAPTER 19

FACING THE END 155

Many feel the absence of courage in facing death as it nears. I explore the philosophical, scientific, and religious ways of confronting my end.

THE AUTHOR 163

INTRODUCTION

To Learn to Die. *Let us disarm him of his novelty and strangeness, let us converse and be familiar with him, and have nothing so frequent in our thoughts as death. Upon all occasions represent him to our imagination in his every shape . . . and thereupon, let us encourage and fortify ourselves.*

Michel de Montaigne, essay, circa 1580

During the course of our lives we prepare for college, careers, marriage, child-rearing, retirement. Why not death? People typically avoid discussing or thinking about the topic because they may regard it as creepy, morbid, macabre or tasteless, or maybe fended off by not contemplating it. But there's mounting evidence that people who engage in such discourse are less depressed and less anxious. Such was the conviction over four hundred years ago of the French philosopher Montaigne, and today the contemplation of life's end could well help some sixty million Americans. That's the number of baby boomers who will die in the next thirty years. If you were born between 1944 and 1964, factually you are a lot closer to death.

Little wonder that more people are reading books about it. Among the bestsellers are Dr. Atul Gawande's *Being Mortal*, which deals with how doctors fail patients at the end of life, and how they can do better. Paul Kalanithi's *When Breath Becomes Air* is an account of the doctor confronting his own death. Neurosurgeon Eben Alexander's *Proof of Heaven* has excited the imagination of millions of readers wanting to know if there's an afterlife. The precursor of these books is *How We Die* by the Yale surgery professor Sherwin B. Nuland, published in 1993.

While some of these and similar books are confessions of people confronting terminal diseases, most of them are by doctors writing about such people. We learn what it's like to suffer varied cancers—brain, pancreatic, lung, colon, stomach, leukemia. The authors describe dying from cardiac failure, HIV, extreme Alzheimer's, and more.

Not much disease and pain will be found in the book you've just opened. Rather, I address topics of death mostly absent in the bestsellers mentioned above—young men taunting death, time perception, the writing of obituaries, near-death experiences, philosophical choices in confronting life's end. At age ninety, I've lived thirty years longer than typical authors of popular books on dying. Thirty years adds a lot of perspective on old-age life, and how to deal with its certain conclusion.

In the pages of this book I meet with a remorseful murderer, and with a prisoner having a piercing vision of time's meaning. I tell about editing and publishing a manual for a test predicting a person's potential for suicide, created by the psychiatrist Humphry Osmond who coined the word psychedelic. I think of what I've written as a worthy intellectual adventure, at worst a foolish scheme. The book's title refers to the three words employed by my father when he sent a telegram to me in England in 1951 as I was boarding a schooner sailing to the South China Sea in search of Captain William Kidd's treasure: "ABANDON FOOLISH SCHEME." I ignored my father's advice, and was almost killed in the process.

I have ceaselessly pursued the study of philosophy since the age of eighteen. In the latter chapters of the book I address the philosophical and religious choices available in confronting the inevitable, and speculation on the afterlife. I write about what groups of aging people are discussing as their end nears; hospice training; planning funerals and memorial services; and the oddity of grieving more about the death of one's pet dog than of one's own parent.

I've spent fifty years editing print magazines, witnessing a cycle of their dying and replacement, and finally what appears to be something like a mass extinction. As the editor of a daily business newspaper I became a statistics fanatic. A single economic index, as I observe in Chapter 6, is leading to the migration, starvation, and tragic deaths of millions. And yet statistically, the world is a safer place than it was a thousand years ago, even though hundreds of thousands of people die annually in violent warfare.

I write about young men taunting death. What value is there in voluntarily risking one's life in dangerous exploits? While I was composing *Abandon Foolish Scheme*, Steven Gubser, one of the world's leading theoretical physicists, fell to his death while climbing a dangerous rock needle next to Mont Blanc in the French Alps. A string theorist, he was close to reconciling the differences between General Relativity and the behavior of subatomic particles. The world may have been deprived of the "explanation of everything" because its potential discoverer lost his life pursuing his recreation of rock climbing—something I came near to doing.

I'm not an especially morose person, neither am I suffocating in dark thoughts. I can be accused perhaps of writing about death in the manner of a dilettante and adventurer, so as to be amusing or entertaining. In any case, I've done so while managing to offer unusual, useful practical advice.

"To study philosophy is to learn to die," proclaimed Montaigne. This book, informed by eight decades of living, adds measurably to the great French *philosophe's* thinking.

CHAPTER 1

NDE

The Near-Death Experience

When death comes...
I want to step through the door full of curiosity, wondering:
what is it going to be like, that cottage of darkness?
"When Death Comes," Mary Oliver

One way to live more meaningfully is to nearly have your life end. It happened to me. As in descriptions of near-death experiences encountered by others, I felt separated from my body. My heart briefly stopped beating. Breathing, or the awareness of it, ceased; I felt myself to be in a place it wasn't needed. Voices sounded distant, exerted no influence, had no emotional impact. I felt no concern or worry about what would happen next.

Although I've experienced it twice in sleep, absent for me was the sensation of being whisked up or through a tunnel toward a benign white light, a common experience of people who come close to dying. Nor did I have another experience that some NDErs have, in which major events in the not-yet-dead person's life are reviewed, or relived, like a film in slow motion. More tranquil sensations happily swept my consciousness.

In the discovery of a world that may lie beyond us, conventional sense of time vanishes. Einstein's notion of time as relative feels like it is being experienced. The duality of things—like good and bad, right and wrong—disappears, or is transcended. The experience is akin to the ability of mystics to suffuse their minds in the timeless, to inhabit a place where past, present, and future are one, where the border between life and death seems permeable, like the cloth that shields skin from air.

When the NDEr is back inside their body, it is nearly always a gross disappointment. The survivor longs to return to the peaceful state of dying where, paradoxically, life was better.

The experience cannot fully be expressed in words. People know it who are adept in the meditative practice of emptying the mind. If you lack that skill, music helps. Crazy as it is for a writer to suggest, the buyer or borrower of this book at this moment might briefly stop reading it. Switch on whatever audio device is at hand, sit in a restful, tranquil position, and play your favorite calming music. I like to listen to Judy Collins's soaring rendition of "Amazing Grace,"

Pachelbel's *Canon in D*, and Simon and Garfunkel singing "The Sounds of Silence."

One is now better disposed to read about dying.

For most scientists, the sublime sensations experienced in nearly dying are merely a result of electrochemical brain activity. They are not unlike the sublime sensations felt when listening to Mozart, or my standing on a mountain gazing at snowcapped peaks reaching skyward. Why this miracle occurs is unknown. Many are inclined to believe that science at some time will have an explanation for it all . . . a not unreasonable claim, given the history of science overturning religion-based theological constructs.

What we think to be consciousness or awareness or self, it is said, is merely the sensation resulting from electrical and chemical interactions of neurons. The process of dying is the gradual cessation of this electrochemical activity . . . or, in nearly dying, its arrest. There is a measurable excess buildup of carbon dioxide in the blood. Finally, in death, the myriad neurons and synapses in our cabbage-like brains cease to function.

"You need blood flow to supply the nutrients to fire the neurons," says Dr. Robert Spetzler director of the Barrow Neurological Institute. "As a scientist, I would say that during hypothermic cardiac arrest, it is inconceivable that any brain function is going on." EEG is completely flat.

Yet Spetzler was puzzled after he operated on the singer and songwriter Pam Reynolds, who was clinically dead during surgery. Reynolds was able to describe objects and recall events that had occurred during her surgery, which could only have been witnessed by someone alive. Her experience, while uncommon, is similar to that of other NDErs. An event takes place that the "dead" person cannot see, but which, to everyone's amazement, they describe following recovery.

"I do not understand from a physiological perspective how that could possibly happen," said Dr. Spetzler. "From a scientific perspective, there is no acceptable explanation." However, in a Canadian Intensive Care Unit, a patient whose life support was turned off showed persistent brain activity. The brain of a clinically dead individual, who lived to tell the tale of his or her NDE, did not cease functioning.

Science is stumped. A near-death experience cannot be measured or directly observed from the outside. Yet people who have returned from the threshold of death tell extraordinary tales that traditional scientific method cannot explain. They write books that sell in the millions.

After two centuries of religion combating science and losing ground, science here is losing ground. Scientists, whose method of thinking is riveted to hypothesis-research-proof methodology, are getting beaten about the ears. Worse for them, in this battle of words and ideas, religionists and spiritualists have the powerful support of the authors of bestselling books, asserting that people who've had the ethereal experience of dying and returning to life, have visited a nonphysical world. Science be damned.

That said, there exists a cadre of scientists and medical professionals who have come to accept that science is limited in what it can observe. Some even believe in the actuality of the immaterial. Dutch cardiologist Pim van Lommel, author of *Consciousness Beyond Life*, firmly says that "consciousness can be experienced independently of brain function," that at the time of physical death consciousness continues to be experienced in another dimension.

For those who have experienced the final stage of exiting life and come back to tell the story, the adventure is contradictory in nature. "There is a triumphant feeling of buoyancy," says my friend Ptolemy Tompkins, author of the bestselling *The Modern Book of the Dead*, "the movement up into other worlds of continually intensifying beauty and strangeness; and the final, resigned return to the abandoned body, going back into which is like climbing into a heap of freezing wet clothes."

"Brain activity isn't consciousness," he says, "and all attempts at finding a neural basis for it have come up with nothing."

Tompkins for many years worked for the mass-circulation magazine founded by Norman Vincent Peale, Guideposts, whose offices are located not far from where I live. Part of his job was to find people who'd had near-death experiences and to write about them for Guideposts two-million-and-more readers. The work eventually led him to write *The Modern Book of the Dead*, published in 2012.

In the near-death experience, says Tompkins, we perceive ourselves in many places at once, similar to the manner in which subatomic particles that only appear to be in one place at a time are in fact in multiple places simultaneously. The dying person thus enters a world increasingly accepted as real by physicists studying the behavior of subatomic particles.

"Science," writes Tompkins, "has in the last century or so, slowly but surely been giving us back our license to . . . think of ourselves as more—much more—than the physical bodies we inhabit while alive."

Consciousness climbs into the brain from outside. Or our brain can be thought of as a kind of TV set displaying in us one spectrum of a universal consciousness that's out there, an idea explored in Chapter 18. The brain dies, consciousness does not. Beyond our skins, consciousness exists.

I once experienced it. During my undergraduate years at McGill University, between 1947 and 1951, I worked in the summer months as a bellhop at the castle-like Banff Springs Hotel in the Rocky Mountains of Alberta, Canada, ferrying guests' luggage from their cars to their rooms. At a staff party, at age eighteen, I had my first experience with hard liquor. I drank a nearly lethal amount of sweet cherry brandy. After vomiting, I staggered back to the employee dormitory.

I lay on my bunk bed, staring at the mattress overhead. Then I passed out.

Whenever now I imagine what my final minutes of life may resemble, this memory fills my mind. I had ceased breathing.

"I don't hear him breathing," echoed voices around and near my head. They were excited, alarmed, believing they were watching someone die.

It didn't matter what they said. I was utterly tranquil, limpid, lacking desire to move arms or legs, blissful.

A voice called out, "The nurse is here!" I felt fingers touch my forehead, then grip my wrist searching for a pulse. I was not breathing. No breath was needed. I was in a place where something else had taken over my life, where I felt no desire to control. I felt totally at peace, ready to go.

To where? To what place?

A thought flickered in my mind. Maybe departing life isn't a good idea. I had plans to ski the glacier. To climb. To go back to college to study philosophy. To bike through Europe. It's not my time. No, I don't want to go.

I willed my lungs to act again. I inhaled through my wide-open mouth a draft of the dormitory's stale air. My hands moved. I twisted my feet. I opened my eyes to find friends' faces staring down at me. I smiled. They smiled.

I'd had a complete sensory experience of what my final moments may resemble.

Back at the hotel, when I recovered the next day, I realized that I'd done something scandalous. I'd been drunk, immature. The manager might terminate my summer employment. At the same time, I'd experienced something sweet and peaceful. There had been no terror. I had been lying comfortably on a bed, doped up, friends around me to say goodbye. I was no longer frightened or terrorized by the prospect of death.

But dying wouldn't be peaceful if one drowned at sea, or were buried in an avalanche, pursued by a bear, or if climbing a cliff the rope broke and one fell into an abyss. Or crashed against boulders in a ski descent. Bone would be crushed, flesh torn. There'd be no tranquil easing from life.

(For more on NDE, visit **iands.org**, the website for the International Association for Near Death Studies.)

CHAPTER 2

FALLING

When young, death is something that happens to other people,
until in the blink of an eye it is there.

In this short span
between my fingertips on the smooth edge
and these tense feet cramped on the crystal ledge
I hold the life of man.
Geoffrey Winthrop Young, "The Cragsman"

A ninety-year-old's mind is suffused with the awareness life is going to end sometime soon, or within the next ten years. You can accept it, be afraid, maybe angry. For me, the awareness of it was scarcely softened recently when I asked a money advisor at Fidelity Investments when his plan assumed I would die. Turning to his computer, he spent a few minutes checking. "Age ninety-five," he announced. I will die within five years of this book's publication.

Seven decades ago, my perspective was markedly different. Like most nineteen-year-olds, I thought of death as something that happens to other people.

Retreating to age three, the idea of death—that life, having just begun, is something that ends—is likely a deeply wounding experience. Such a childish epiphany, triggered perhaps by attending a funeral with parents, or a glimpse of dying bodies next to a crushed automobile, may be so traumatic that the child instantly represses it. The repression may be sublimated in some later-in-life personality quirk, like ignoring death, or writing a book about it!

As a teenager, in deep bouts of depression and lack of confidence, I was not alone in occasionally thinking of committing suicide; it's the second leading cause of death among juveniles fifteen to nineteen years of age. Otherwise, in my teenage mind, the possibility of dying was a subtle, minor, mostly unconsidered component of the excitement of risk-taking. Fatality was seen as an unlikely outcome of risky adventures, and easy to deny that it could ever happen.

Outside the dormitory in Banff where I'd had my near-death experience looms the 9,672-foot peak of Mount Rundle. The mountain is admired by guests who book a Banff Springs Hotel room with a view, and it's a familiar image on postcards sold in the hotel lobby gift shop.

Like the in-run of a ski jump in the sky, Rundle's southern side slopes gradually and gently downwards from its peak.

The northern side is a gigantic cliff. It was in my face every day, like a bully inviting me to fight. I determined to climb it.

I had no training in rock climbing at the time. A couple of years later, in the Adirondacks, I had a brief lesson from Fritz Wiessner, who made climbing history in 1938 by almost completing the first ascent of the world's second-highest mountain, K2. Wiessner taught me a few moves, grips, reminded me to keep my upper body away from the rock, how to belay another climber. It was knowledge that at this moment I only crudely possessed from having read books. But I had no doubt that I could successfully climb the four-thousand vertical feet of Rundle's cliff. From below the summit, I calculated, I'd be able to amble easily down the southern slope back to the hotel dormitory where we lived, and where I'd recently experienced what it might be like to die.

On a day off from work I persuaded Swede, a taciturn, solidly built Albertan, and his athletic waitress girlfriend Helen to join me. Long on adventure, short on technical skills, we set out to the base of the cliff, bearing knapsacks containing water bottles and sandwiches. I carried a hundred-foot length of manila rope that I'd bought in the local hardware store. It was nylon, made in Delaware.

After an hour of steepening ascent through light brush and boulders, we encountered the first vertical rise requiring serious foot- and handholds. I reached up for the first handhold on the small ledge of a seemingly firm piece of rock. In an instant the limestone detached from my hand, toppled from the cliff, whistled down, narrowly missing my friends below. Suddenly we'd learned why experienced climbers didn't frequent Rundle's precipitous backside: it was a mass of rotten rock.

So far the climbing hadn't been especially forbidding. Just carefully test each handhold for the solidity of the rock. Higher and higher we climbed until we found ourselves on a spacious ledge. Rundle's summit was three or four hundred vertical feet above. To reach it we would have to circle around for an easier ascent on the mountain's western slope. It would mean scaling and traversing an exposed rock face with little below it but air. Hand- and footholds looked to be plentiful, I thought, but how trustworthy was the rock?

I volunteered to lead the way. The hardware-store rope was tied snugly around my waist. For belay I had looped the other end of it around the thick trunk of a dwarf spruce tree firmly rooted on the ledge. Swede fed the rope as I climbed. My aim was to reach a long, widening ledge that would take us around to safety.

Gradually I made my way up, once dislodging a sliver of rock that might have served as a handhold. I stared down at the falling rock as it clip-clopped, chip-chipped on the cliff's knobby face, disappearing into the chasm below.

There was no possibility of retreat now, I realized . . . of descending back to my friends. The immediate goal was a broad, walkable ledge six feet above me. A couple of feet below it was a stratum or layer of rock whose upper edge offered a handhold. I found a solid place for one steel hobnailed boot to stand on. How I wished I'd worn rubber-soled sneakers that might have adhered better to the rock. But my real and urgent concern now was whether or not the layer of rock would peel off the face when I grabbed it with my hand. The result would likely be fatal. I'd have a fall of about seventy-five feet before the rope would tighten around my waist. If it didn't break, I'd be hanging helplessly over the abyss. If the rope broke or the knot in it failed, I would plunge to a certain death.

There was no way out except upward. I extended my right arm up, grabbed the top edge of the rock layer. The rock held! Swiftly I moved my right leg up and across, found the foothold, pushed up, grabbed the ledge with my other hand, and hurled my body onto the wide platform, the path to safety.

I'd escaped death by falling, but not the terrifying nightmare that still occasionally invades my sleeping head. My hand reaches up, not knowing if the rock will break off, leaving my body to hurtle down into the abyss. In the dream, my hand never reaches the rotten rock. I awake, my body bathed in sweat, whimpering in my throat.

My experience on Mount Rundle bears an eerie resemblance to a climbing experience of the famous physician and pain specialist Hans Kraus when he was a teenager. Doctor Kraus in later life prescribed the physical therapy that saved me from back surgery. His dear friend was Fritz Wiessner, who gave me my first climbing lesson. Illustrious among Dr. Kraus's patients were Eleanor Roosevelt, President John F. Kennedy, actresses Greta Garbo, Lauren Bacall, Rita Hayworth and Katherine Hepburn, radio broadcaster Lowell Thomas, actors Yul Brynner and Danny Kaye, and dozens of other celebrities. I commissioned Kraus to write in Ski magazine about injuries, and about the Kraus Weber fitness test that he had created during Dwight Eisenhower's presidency. In his latter years Kraus and his wife Madi, both superb skiers, became my friends.

In the Austrian Alps, when he was seventeen, Kraus set off with his friend Marcus to do a first serious climb. At the time, he was living and studying in Switzerland, where his father had hired James Joyce to tutor him in English.

The boys were ridiculously equipped. Hans wore espadrilles, and Marcus only heavy socks. They had a rope, but no pitons to secure it to. In her account of the climb, Susan E.B. Schwartz, author of Kraus's well-deserved biography *JFK's Secret Doctor*, relates that "the boys agreed that if the leader fell, the other would try to catch him by yanking the rope tight and bracing against the rock."

It was "unconscionable, completely irresponsible," Kraus recalled, "but you do stupid things when you're young."

The teenagers reached a small ledge, barely big enough to accommodate the two of them and the coiled rope. To ascend the last precipitous pitch before the summit, Marcus led the way, the rope attached to his waist. Up from the ledge the rock above bulged out, so that Hans lost sight of his friend. He could tell by the rope paying out, though, that Marcus was making upward progress.

"I heard Marcus pant," Kraus recalled in Schwartz's account of what happened. "Then I heard him call out, 'It's very hard, but I'll try it. In few more meters I'll be at the next ledge, and then it's easy going to the top.'

"All of a sudden," Kraus said, "I heard a scream. Then a terrific crash. Blocks of rock were falling down. Then there was a smell I'll never forget: nauseating, acrid, like sulfur. I saw a rock falling down. And I saw Marcus falling down, too, straight over my head.

"I called out to him, 'I can hold you, Marcus. I can hold you.'" But the rope kept slithering through Hans's hands, ninety feet or more of it, faster and faster. Finally the tail end of the rope slipped through his hands, and he watched as it disappeared down the mountain.

Alone now, Hans was stranded on the narrow ledge, without a rope, hundreds of feet above the ground. Looking back more than seventy years, he recalled to Schwartz that he entered a trance-like state, under a kind of self-hypnosis, the hot sun beating down. One day, he reflected, he too would die. Or maybe what had happened was all a mirage. Maybe Marcus was okay. How could death have come so quickly, without reason or warning, for someone so young and strong?

Then Hans began his own descent. It would be perilous, dangerous in the extreme, with no rope to save him from a mistake.

Focusing minutely on each movement of a hand and a foot, he made his way down. As he drew closer to the base, he spotted his friend.

"Marcus was lying on his back with his head down the slope," Kraus recalled. "Or what was left of his head. Everything was bashed in. There was blood everywhere. I leaned over and pressed my ear to his chest. There was no sound, no heartbeat."

For the first time, Hans noticed his own hands. They were one big, oozing wound. In trying to save Marcus by grabbing and holding the rope, he had burned the skin off his hands down to raw bone.

The next day, a rescue crew brought Marcus's body back to the village. He was buried next to the church. In his old age, Kraus never forgot. "For the rest of his life," writes Schwartz, "he would break his life into two parts: Before Marcus and After Marcus."

Like Kraus and countless others I know, I nearly died in accidents of my own creation. In a split second, at high speed, or driving toward a giant truck or a tree, the awareness of death is sudden . . . not as now, in old age, when death is felt as a gradually approaching event. When young I don't recall thinking much about it, except that it was something that happened to others, until in the blink of an eye it was there. Years after my experience on Mount Rundle I discovered what may have been an inward, mental outcome of the climb, expressed in the poet Christian Wiman's transformative book *My Bright Abyss*.

"Part of my enjoyment of life," writes Wiman, "has always been an unconscious assumption of its continuity. We live in a land where only other people die. We cannot imagine our own death until it is thrust upon us."

Through the episodes of nearly dying when I was young, a new direction may have been given to my life. What direction it gave, however, I know no more than I know how much my character was shaped by the traumatic passage from my mother's womb into the world.

CHAPTER 3

CRASHING

"What madness it is to expect to die of that failing of our powers brought on by extreme old age . . . when it is the least usual, the rarest kind of death . . . . We call that death a natural death, as if it were unnatural to find a man breaking his neck in a fall, engulfed in a shipwreck, surprised by a plague or pleurisy."

Michel de Montaigne (circa 1580)

I am not a war veteran. I've not been at risk of dying from a bullet or shrapnel wound. I was too young to serve in World War II, was living in Canada at the time of the Korean War, and was too old to be drafted for Vietnam. My close encounters with death have come not from being ordered into battle, but from voluntary choice of challenge. Death suffered as a result of following one's own command is different from following another's.

But there's a common denominator, too, felt by veteran soldier and risk-taking adventurer alike. The raw fear is felt as intensely, or even more so, not at the moment of nearly getting killed—at the time one was actually in peril—but years later. A war veteran experiences it in the form of post-traumatic stress disorder. Blood pressure rises, accompanied by sweating. Long after combat, a Vietnam veteran may recall the gruesome wounding and dying of a blood-spattered fellow soldier next to him. Now, in old age, he relives the experience. My brushes with death exist in nightmares that wake me from sleep, my heart palpitating.

A year after my ill-advised climb and NDE at Banff, I found myself on New Year's Eve among a half-dozen McGill University ski team members on the 2,870-foot summit of Mont Tremblant in Quebec's Laurentians. We were camped in a cabin loaned to us by Tremblant's millionaire American owner Joseph Bondurant Ryan.

The day of slalom training and lift-riding had been warm and rainy. By nightfall, though, a brutal cold swept in from Hudson's Bay. The temperature plummeted to forty degrees below zero Fahrenheit. Inside the cabin a watch was maintained to ensure that someone was stoking the flames of the wood-burning, cast-iron, potbellied stove. Ski boots were placed in a ring around the stove so that the leather didn't freeze.

Waking in the morning, as I walked outside to pee my feet slid out from under me, and I fell on my back. I was lying on a virtual hockey rink. The warmed, wet snow of yesterday was now a thick crust of ice. The entire mountain had become a glacier, scintillating in the light of the rising arctic sun. The cable and seats of the chairlift were so heavily encased in ice that the lift could not function. Getting off the mountain was going to be a dangerous exercise.

By midmorning the outside temperature had risen to zero degrees Fahrenheit. Leaving the cabin on seven-foot wood skis, like the others, I began the descent, sidestepping my skis. Each lateral step involved smashing the downhill ski into the icy crust in order to break it up. We took off our skis in places and kicked steps into the ice with our boots. Needed was enough of a purchase on the steep slope to prevent sliding out of control. Failure would lead to a faster and faster glissade down the mountain, with the serious if not mortal risk of crashing headfirst into a tree at high speed. It took us three hours to descend the mountain's 2,000 vertical feet, typically a ten-minute descent on skis.

Four months later I found myself climbing and skiing on the headwall of the steepest, most dangerous slope east of the Rockies, Tuckerman Ravine on Mount Washington in New Hampshire. Going to Tuckerman in the springtime was a ritual for college students, and still is. After writing April exams at McGill University, I made the trip with three other students in a Packard, the trunk stuffed with camping gear, skis mounted on the roof rack. On the long drive southeastward, the car radio blared the big-band music of Harry James, Glenn Miller and Artie Shaw.

Approaching from the west, New Hampshire's Presidential Range appeared to us as a vast 4,000-foot-high forested line filling the sky. Mounts Madison, Adams, and Jefferson rise only a few hundred feet above the 5,000-foot-high ridge that connects them. Mount Washington, though, is easily spotted. At 6,288 feet, the highest in northeastern North America, it stands above the others, its massive bald dome scarred by buildings sprouting television, radio, and weather antennae. A broadcasting tower atop the Matterhorn could not look uglier.

On the mountain's concealed eastern side is Tuckerman Ravine, somewhat misnamed in that it is not really a ravine, but rather a huge glacial cirque, horseshoe in shape. All winter long it receives massive clouds of snow blown off Mt. Washington's exposed western side by world-record velocity winds. The snow cascades like a Niagara Falls down into the ravine. Deep by as much as a hundred feet, the fallen snow makes skiing possible into July.

Arriving at Pinkham Notch, we parked the car next to the Appalachian Mountain Club (AMC) camp house. Filling our packs with clothing, food, and beer, we lashed skis to our pack frames and started the four-mile climb on the Fire Trail up to the Harvard Hut. Although it was under the care of the Harvard Mountaineering Club, the hut in winter was mostly occupied by Dartmouth, Middlebury, and McGill skiers. The compact interior smelled of drying clothes and of molten paraffin ski wax. I threw my sleeping bag onto one of a half-dozen hard-surfaced wooden bunk beds.

From the hut in the morning I set out for the Headwall, skis on shoulder, passing the lean-tos and tents pitched around a large shelter built by the Civilian Conservation Corps in 1936, comically named the Howard Johnson. After climbing the Little Headwall, I reached the ravine floor. Above, a U-shaped sweep of snow and rock etched the skyline.

The Headwall is so steep that standing sideways you can extend one arm out and almost touch the slope. Up and up I climbed, placing my leather boots into the steps made by previous climbers. Reaching a point under a cliff, where no further climbing was possible, I kicked the snow into a narrow platform, onto which I laid my almost seven-foot-long wooden skis. Precariously perched, I managed to get my boots into the bindings, known as "bear traps" because they didn't release your foot in a fall. I was ready for the descent.

There was little room for error. If someone falls on the Headwall, his or her spread-eagled body cascades over the wet corn-snow like a trash bag tumbling down a steep ramp. Skis remained attached to legs. If a wooden ski didn't break, your leg did.

A skier who failed to make a turn to check his speed could find his skis headed straight down. It happened to Austrian champion Toni Matt in the 1939 Inferno Race from the summit of Mt. Washington 3.8 miles down to Pinkham Notch. Up on the snowfield above the Headwall, Matt made two or three turns, decided he should be going faster. By the time he dropped over the lip into the ravine he was already going so fast he was unable to make another turn to slow his speed. He had no choice but to point his seven-foot-three-inch hickory skis straight down. He rocketed down the Headwall, and managed to cross the smooth floor of the ravine without falling, entering the wooded trail that led to the bottom.

In an attempt to explain what had happened to him, Matt later joked, "I was nineteen, stupid, and had strong legs." His Headwall schuss became an American skiing legend. It was similar to the partial Headwall descent I was about to make, in that it was unintended.

I grabbed my poles, and with a hop directed my skis downhill. I quickly made the first in a planned series of short, hard turns, jamming the edges into the snow to control my speed. But in making the second turn, I let my feet go forward too much, my body fell back. By the time I was rebalanced on my skis they were headed straight down. I accelerated so suddenly that I decided there was no choice but to stand up and continue the schuss. I was rocketing straight down. I had no sense of time. Everything seemed to be happening in slow motion. Then I hit the transition to the gently sloping ravine floor. Its surface was not the smooth snow that had enabled Matt to survive. It was rough washboard. My skis chattered uncontrollably. My whole body was vibrating like an automobile traveling over cobblestone. Ahead I spotted a pair of boulders protruding from the snow. To avoid crashing into them, in a desperate attempt to turn, I twisted my skis sideways. My edges caught on the rough granular ice, causing my body to be hurled into the air. As if by a miracle, I flew over the top of the boulders.

When I opened my eyes, the world was upside down. My still-attached skis were suspended in a thicket of saplings, my boots ensnared in the branches, my head hung down near the snow.

It had happened to me at noon observed by a hundred skiers seated in a place called the Lunch Rocks on the Ravine's floor. They cheered loudly in appreciation of the astonishing crash they'd just observed. Two came over to help me untangle my skis from the thicket. I thanked them, glided across the floor of the Ravine, took off my skis, and began to climb the steep slope to make another descent.

Getting up from a fall and undertaking the same risk again can be said to be a mark of courage and success. Not doing so is failure. When the person fails to get up because he died, it's called an accident.

CHAPTER 4

BURIED

"The fear of death follows from the fear of life. A man who lives fully is prepared to die at any time."

Mark Twain

In the mountains are two among several ways of getting killed. Both are sudden in their happening, but can lead to agonizingly slow deaths. One is to fall into a crevasse. The other is burial in an avalanche.

On a slope, roughly of the steepness of a black-diamond run at a ski area, a skier or climber may accidentally cause snow, lying on an unstable surface, to break off. The volume of snow grows in size as it falls, a mass accelerating on a steep slope to fifty-mile-an-hour speeds and faster. The avalanche accumulates more snow as it descends. Anyone unfortunate enough to be on the slope below, in its path, is catapulted into a monstrous, dense cloud.

At the bottom of the slope, where the ground flattens, the avalanche slows, then arrests as a vast mound of pressurized snow, compacted like cement. The victim buried inside it is unable to move their arms and their hands to clear the snow from around the mouth and nostrils, so breathing is impossible. A slow asphyxiation occurs. If rescuers above probing with sticks or detection devices cannot find them and dig them out, the victim, deprived of oxygen, dies in a cold coffin, to be dug up later.

On a glacier, a fatal accident can happen in the midst of delirious play. In an ethereal space where the snow-covered mountains limn the heavens, a skier experiences the glorious feeling of gliding, twisting, flexing and soaring. At high speed, time slows down. A peaceful sensation envelops the skier. Distracted, if he errs in judging his speed, or misses observing a dangerous sign, the perfect run can end abruptly, in a bad way. Concealed from a skier, a snow bridge spans a narrow crevasse. It is a separation or gap in the glacier, which lies hundreds of feet thick over the mountain. The skier doesn't see it. The bridge breaks and he plummets into a cavernous, icy interior, his body ricocheting downward into a space from which there is no escape.

It almost happened to me on a glacier a hundred miles away from where I'd almost fallen off Mount Rundle's precipitous, crumbling backside. Before taking up my summer job again in Banff, I'd driven north to the Columbia Icefields in the company of Doug Pfeiffer, a ski instructor who twenty-five years later the world would recognize as "the father of freestyle skiing." Our plan was to climb as high as the snow would allow on Mount Athabasca, a pyramidal peak of 11,453 feet. The mountain rises above the huge, dirty tongue of the glacier known as the Icefields, the source of the Columbia River.

It was mid-May, the sky cloudless. The sun rising in the east bathed the mountain in dazzling light. The snow was just soft enough to kick footsteps into it with our leather boots. Bearing seven-foot-long skis lashed to pack-frames on our backs, we ascended a vast glacial slope. Sweating from the exertion of climbing under the blazing sun, I stripped to the waist. The light amplified by the snow's whiteness at such an altitude seared my skin. As we climbed, a quarter-mile up, not far to my right, I spotted a shadowy depression in the snow—a zigzag, telltale line, proof of deep snow covering a crevasse. The snow bridge most likely wouldn't bear the pressure of a skier crossing it. Peering farther across the slope, I could glimpse the gaping darkness of the crevasse itself.

Another quarter-mile up we reached the top of the skiable snow. The surface was now of perfect softness for skiing, two inches of velvety cream-cheese-like snow on a hard undersurface. I started down, arcing long, graceful turns by the mere action of cutting my steel-edged skis into the perfect surface. Pfeiffer was to my right and slightly ahead of me. Turn after effortless turn generated an enchanting rhythm that swept uncontrollably over my whole body. As if on a ballroom floor, not wishing the dance ever to end, I continued, senseless of my direction.

Far off, out of the corner of my eye I saw that Pfeiffer had stopped. He was waving his ski pole in the air. Reluctantly I made a final turn, and stopped. I looked down the slope, and realized why he'd been signaling me. I had stopped only fifty yards short of the depression in the snow covering the crevasse. Two more turns and I would have skied onto the snow bridge, which likely would have collapsed. I would have plunged into the icy tomb, my cascading body bouncing from one frozen outcropping to another, hundreds of feet down.

For many years afterwards, I imagined what it would have been like if I'd cascaded into the crevasse. Like the Rundle nightmare, in which my hand reached up to the fatal rock edge wondering if it would hold, it became a dream. I do not see the crevasse. I ski toward the snow bridge, and feel it collapse. I plunge into the frozen interior of the glacier."You wouldn't have survived," the extreme skier Jim McConkey told me years later. "Even if your fall had been arrested like mine, you had no rope and no crampons to effect a rescue."

The year before, a couple of miles away and six miles up the tongue of the Columbia Icefield, McConkey had been working as the camera-carrying member of a crew filming a segment of a never-completed movie, *The Shadow of Time*, for a Hollywood film outfit headed by legendary movie star and director Erick von Stroheim. Much later McConkey told his story to the renowned radio broadcaster Lowell Thomas, and seventy years afterward I discovered and published Thomas's account.

On the glacier, as the film crew was climbing, McConkey lost control of his skis. Desperately skidding and sliding, he struggled to stay above a yawning crevasse. He failed and plunged into the hole. Down he went into it, the sound of his skis rattling, followed by a dull thud, then a low moan. McConkey's fall had been arrested by a massive platform of ice that was jammed like a plug between the two walls of the crevasse. He was at least eighty feet down, his head buried in the snow, skis still attached to his feet. A fast rescue was needed if McConkey were to survive.

One of the skiers performing in the film was Toni Matt, the same guy whose straight-line schuss of the Headwall of Tuckerman Ravine on Mt. Washington I recounted in the previous chapter. The powerfully built Matt donned crampons, roped himself, and rappelled into the icy coffin. Eighty feet down he spotted the red soles of the boots of McConkey, who was buried from the waist in the snow, upside down. Somehow he'd managed to free one hand enough to undo his bindings and detach his skis. But his face was blue from the cold and near-suffocation, and by now both he and Matt were soaked to the skin in freezing water.

"I was in the crevasse for an hour," McConkey recalled, "in and out of consciousness, the pain unbelievable. I was five minutes from dying."

Fifty years later, McConkey told me what it was like.

"Did you pray to God?" I asked.

"You bet I did."

29

"But you once told me you're a confirmed atheist."

"Not then I wasn't," McConkey laughed.

Securing the rope around McConkey, Matt shouted to the men above to start pulling Jim's fractured body upward. Matt repeatedly maneuvered it from below, to get him to the top and into the open air. After an hour, they succeeded. Lashing McConkey to a primitive sledge, they began the agonizing six-mile trip down the crevasse-ridden glacier.

Just as they started down, the men heard a tremendous roar above their heads. They watched helplessly as a block of ice weighing hundreds of tons tumbled down over a rock wall, headed towards them. Miraculously it stopped just 50 feet short of where they were standing with the nearly lifeless McConkey lying on the sledge.

McConkey went on to become an iconic extreme skier, appearing on magazine covers and starring in ski movies. In 1968, in the Bugaboo mountain range of British Columbia, I directed a *Ski* magazine photo shoot in which McConkey is seen vaulting across the kind of crevasse in which he'd almost died eighteen years earlier. Highly intelligent, he was a living contradiction of the familiar adage, "Courage is knowing something can harm, and doing it anyway; stupidity is the same." At age ninety, he was still skiing. Among the most famous action shots of McConkey is one that appeared in *Sports Illustrated*, in which he has triggered an avalanche at Alta, Utah, and is seen outracing it down the mountain.

I once skied through an avalanche myself. In 1964 I'd trekked up to the vast treeless terrain, not far from Aspen, above the ghost town of Ashcroft. With me was Olympic skier Tom Corcoran, who would soon open his Waterville Valley resort in New Hampshire, and his wife Birdie, sister of the actor Sam Waterston. I'd just become editor-in-chief of *Ski* magazine, for which Corcoran was writing a column. Tom's idea of our getting to know one another better was to spend a few days in the backcountry with him and Birdie, skiing above Ashcroft below Pearl Pass, overnighting in the Tagert Hut at 11,000 feet.

A couple of runs into the day we were skiing side by side in fresh bottomless powder. So light the snow, I thought, it's like being in a cloud, the snow bathing my face. Down we went into a shallow gully and up the counter slope, coming to a stop. We looked back. A huge pile of snow had filled the gully. Luckily we were not in it. Way up the slope I could see the fracture line, where we'd triggered the slide. We had just skied through an avalanche . . . without knowing it!

Utilizing several hundred square miles of the Purcell Mountains in British Columbia, Austrian mountain guide Hans Gmoser had created the world's first coordinated hut and helicopter operation for skiers in the Bugaboo range. He opened the new Bugaboo lodge in 1968.

A dozen years later, my close friend and college fraternity brother Geoff Taylor, older brother of the philosopher Charles Taylor, traveled to the Bugaboos. On the second day of Taylor's vacation the helicopter lifted his group of skiers to a high ridge, from which they were to descend a steep open slope of untracked powder snow.

Taylor wanted to photograph them. From the 'copter's landing point atop the ridge, he skied briefly down the slope, making a quick stop turn, so that he could point his camera up at the group. His turn triggered an immense avalanche, totally unanticipated by the guide. Taylor was swept down a thousand feet, lost in a swirl of snow the size of a monstrous cumulus cloud. His body was found hours later, buried deep in the tons of cascading powder, his snow-crammed mouth and nostrils incapable of inhaling oxygen. It was the first death of a paying Canadian Mountain Holidays client, and it dragged Gmoser deeper into the realization that he was engaged in a business that could lead to the tragic deaths of its customers.

Taylor had drowned in snow, not the waters of the English Channel, where he and I had been shipwrecked in 1951. It was an adventure that defined the trajectory of my life and career.

CHAPTER 5

SHIPWRECKED

From the first stir of the air felt on his cheek the gale seemed to take upon itself the accumulated impetus of an avalanche. It was something formidable and swift, like the sudden smashing of a vial of wrath. It seemed to explode all round the ship with an overpowering concussion and a rush of great waters, as if an immense dam had been blown up to windward. An earthquake, a landslip, an avalanche, overtake a man incidentally, as it were—without passion. A furious gale attacks him like a personal enemy, tries to grasp his limbs, fastens upon his mind, seeks to rout his very spirit out of him.

Joseph Conrad, *Typhoon*

ABANDON FOOLISH SCHEME.

Telegram to the author from his father, November 1951.

The year after my nearly lethal crash on Mt. Washington, I graduated from McGill University, Bachelor of Arts 1951. I'd successfully applied to do postgraduate work in philosophy at Edinburgh University. The historic Scottish university had become a center for the study of the works of Soren Kierkegaard, the Danish philosopher, arguably the father of the modern Existentialist movement, whose complexities and profundities I'd attempted to penetrate at McGill.

Before going to Edinburgh, during the summer I worked my way across the Atlantic on a freighter, then bicycled around Belgium, France, Italy, Austria, and Germany. After a seasick crossing from Dieppe, I traveled by train to London. It was early September. In two weeks, I would head north to pursue my master's degree in philosophy. Meanwhile, I was sharing a room in Earl's Court with a Montreal friend and fraternity brother Geoffrey Taylor, whose avalanche death twenty-five years later I described in the previous chapter. That tragedy, on a mountain, was now, almost, to be preceded by one at sea.

In fogbound London one day, as Taylor and I were about to exit the Piccadilly Circus underground station, we spotted a Toronto friend, Ian Rogers, riding the down-escalator.

"Wait for us," we shouted.

"What're you up to?" I asked Rogers when we met. `

"I've joined an expedition to search for Captain Kidd's treasure in the South China Sea."

"What?" I scoffed.

"Yeah, we're sailing on a magnificent schooner. The *Lamorna*. She's a hundred and forty feet long, modeled after the Nova Scotia *Bluenose*. She's moored now on the south coast, in Gosport across from Portsmouth harbor. I'm an investor."

"I don't have the money. What if I wanted to go?"

"Maybe you could work your way on. Go down to Gosport and help the skipper in preparing the ship."

We arranged to meet the next day in a pub. Taylor was wildly enthusiastic. Like Rogers he'd decided to invest in the expedition. And yes, Rogers told me, the schooner's owner and master, the Greek Captain Coumandareos, was willing to take me on, cleaning, scraping, and painting the hull and cabins of his ship *Lamorna*. It would enable me to become a non-investing crew member. The schooner would set sail in early November.

Sailing to the South China Sea to search for Captain William Kidd's treasure! A once-in-a-lifetime opportunity! I repeated to myself. A chance like this will never come again!

I wrote a letter to Edinburgh's Philosophy Department. "*John Fry regrets he has canceled plans to attend the fall semester.*" I'd have to forfeit the deposit made on my tuition. The next day I boarded the train for Portsmouth, and that night I slept in a comfortable bunk, the gentle sound of Solent waters lapping on the moored schooner's hull, in the yard of the historic shipbuilder Camper and Nicholsons. Captain Coumandareos was the only other person on board. At breakfast in the morning he told me more about the expedition plan, now called Lamornaventure. The venture, the captain said, was to profit from making a documentary film about adventurers seeking a treasure. Two cameramen would be on board with us. The documentary of sailing halfway around the world in search of buried gold and silver would be profitably shown in movie theaters.

The chart that would guide us had been found secreted in a chest that once belonged to the privateer Captain William Kidd. Somehow the chest found its way into the possession of Sir Malcolm Campbell, at one time the holder of world speed records on land and sea. Sir Malcolm left the chest to his housekeeper Mrs. Elizabeth Dick, who had discovered in its interior a panel which she pried open. Inside was the map of an island, showing the location of something valuable and buried.

"Now I'm going to tell you a secret that you must never share with anyone except our crew." The aging skipper leaned his wrinkled, olive-hued face toward my ear, and whispered, "The name of the island shown on the chart is Pulau Panjang. At least, that is the explanation I've heard from the Marquis de Videlou-Guimbeau."

The Marquis was an authority on the geography of the Indian Ocean where Kidd and his mutinous crew had captured French ships and looted from them gold, gems, and silks. Determined to meet the Marquis, I took a day off from scraping paint from the *Lamorna*'s cabin top, and rode the train to London where I met him at Claridge's for tea.

"The chart," he said, "predated the existence of longitude. But it does show the island's latitude. I simply circled the globe on that latitude, looking for an island shaped like the one on Kidd's map. It was in the Java Sea, which is connected by a strait to the South China Sea. Captain Kidd never sailed there, so I assume the chart was the original property of someone else."

"From what I've read of your Lamornaventure," continued the Marquis, with a mocking smile, "the press is intentionally misrepresenting your expedition." He was right. Lamornaventure was not an expedition expected to find Kidd's legendary trove of silver and gems that he accumulated when he was capturing ships in the Indian Ocean in 1698. Kidd had managed to get the loot to Madagascar, and then across the Atlantic, possibly to the West Indies and eventually to New York's Long Island Sound. But now, as we prepared in England for our voyage, the mass-circulation tabloid papers were falsely promoting the idea that Captain Kidd's long-lost treasure would finally be found.

Indeed, when I returned to the boat from London, a tabloid news photographer was waiting at dockside. He dressed Taylor and me in pirate's garb, Taylor's left eye covered by a black patch. Between us he placed a shapely eighteen-year-old actress in a bathing suit, who'd just appeared in her first film. She was Joan Collins. The picture occupied a half-page in the *Daily Mail* and the cover of *Weekend Magazine* in Montreal, embarrassing our scandalized parents, who were compelled agonizingly to explain to their friends how their sons had managed to become so unserious about their lives.

Most of the fourteen men who would manage the *Lamorna's* canvas and rigging, like myself, were sailing novices, with the exception of the cook who would prepare our meals, and had done so on other ships. One investor was a landlubbing ice-cream vendor who'd used his life savings to join the expedition. Coumandareos, a master of steamships, himself had limited experience in commanding a large sailing vessel like the *Lamorna*. He had made operating her less challenging though. She carried far less canvas than when she'd sailed competitively fifty years earlier in the Cowes Regatta. And Coumandareos had added a diesel engine.

On the eve of leaving Gosport, a bicycle-riding messenger arrived dockside, and handed me a telegram. I could see it was from Canada. I quickly tore it open, and immediately read these four words: ABANDON FOOLISH SCHEME. – FATHER.

Well, Dad, I thought, it's too late.

After two months of preparation, we motored into the English Channel on November 2, 1951. Around the eastern end of the Isle of Wight, Coumandareos ordered us to raise sail. Against the prevailing westerly winds he initiated a series of diagonal crossings aimed at taking the schooner westward out of the Channel, and down the French coast toward Spain and Africa.

After one night of sailing, at the end of a long southwest tack, the

Normandy coast came into view. *Lamorna* went around and tacked northwest, the wind freshening. Topsail was lowered, jib withdrawn. The wind began to whistle in the rigging. Ominous emerald and inky green waves, flecked with white spray at their peaks, grew in size. The English Channel is notably treacherous for ships when high winds coalesce with its powerful tidal currents, varying shallowness, and the funnel-like narrowing of the Channel's width. On its surface a gale storm can have a hurricane-like effect. Rocks, sandbanks, and shoals are a constant threat, as well.

To prevent the schooner going abeam of the mounting waves, Coumandareos ordered me as helmsman, on one watch, to keep *Lamorna* headed up into the wind. When he spotted a tangled halyard line, I volunteered to climb the mainmast to free it. The view from on high was exhilarating, the graceful shape of the *Lamorna*'s hull below, riding on the sea's surface. But I failed at the task of disentangling the snarled line, and descended to the deck to resume my post at the wheel. One crew member called me a hero. In truth, I wasn't. It was simply a case of relieving my anxiety by doing something. Climbing the mast and working at the helm were less stressful than doing nothing.

In the ensuing several hours a constant, violent luffing of the main and foresails shook the ship to her beams. Seated in the cockpit, I saw the peak halyard suddenly detach from the *Lamorna*'s massive mainmast. The crew fled below as the separated gaff and the canvas of the mainsail collapsed onto the boom and onto the deck.

Sail could no longer power the schooner. Coumandareos ordered the engineer to start the diesel engine. But the huge waves lifted the engine's water-cooling intake into the air. The dry, overheated engine seized up and shut down. The schooner was adrift. The waves were now of a monstrous height. I watched from the cockpit as a wave that looked as high as fifty feet towered over us. Surely it will swamp the whole ship, I thought. The *Lamorna*'s bow thrust toward the sky, and we rode over the wave's crest.

The wind was pushing us in the direction of the Needles, jagged rocks at the Isle of Wight's western end, the cause of shipwrecks and loss of lives over the years. Below deck our radioman tapped out an SOS appeal for help.

Within hours of radioing our distress, the Royal Navy sloop *HMS Redpole* appeared. "Prepare to receive tow line," announced a voice over a loudspeaker. I could see a sailor on the destroyer's deck ready to hurl a line to *Lamorna*. But as *Redpole* came closer a monster wave swung the *Lamorna*'s bowsprit against her bow, smashing it and loosening the lines attached to the schooner's foremast. At the same moment, the towrope landed on our deck. Rogers grabbed it, and began to loop it over a capstan on the Lamorna's deck. "No, no, not around the capstan," shouted the loudspeaker voice. "No, no, tie it around the foremast." Bad decision.

As *Redpole* powered ahead, the heavy tow line popped out of the sea and tightened. The powerful towing action now pulled the

Lamorna's bow down into a massive wave. I heard a noise like a cannon shot. The force of the towing was so great that the foremast, lacking the support of the stays from the bowsprit, broke and fell sternwards with a crash, bringing the mainmast down with it. A monstrous snarled mass of rigging, masts and canvas now completely covered the deck.

Lamorna had in seconds become scarcely more than a wreck of a hull. HMS *Redpole* continued towing so that the wind and waves wouldn't carry us onto Needles at the western end of the Isle of Wight. But another solution was needed. Fear spread among our crew. A feeling of helplessness united with hopelessness suffused my mind. I felt numb. Here I was, twenty-one years old, aboard a controlless schooner rising up, sinking down in the waves, and maybe this was going to be the end of a short life. I had not accomplished much. I'd stupidly not gone to Edinburgh to study. I'd spent my teenage years often fighting my father's wishes. I hadn't heeded his plea telegraphed to me the day before we sailed out of Portsmouth harbor: He'd been right, after all. I had become involved in a foolish scheme, had made a spectacularly bad decision. I had failed him and myself. I berated myself through the night (and over the ensuing months, becoming deeply depressed).

By evening hopes rose. *HMS Redpole* had succeeded in attracting a rescue launch to come out from the Isle of Wight. As the lifeboat approached it spread oil on the water to calm the heavy, breaking seas, but without much effect. Getting alongside *Lamorna* was complicated because of the floating spars and debris hanging off the schooner's side. Finally the lifeboat's crew were able to loosely attach lines connecting the two vessels. One by one, ordered by our rescuers, we were to jump off the schooner's deck onto their deck, about eight feet below. The jump was challenging because the turbulence of the sea caused the gap between the two boats to widen and narrow haphazardly. A rope was attached to my waist, but of what use would it be in that dark narrow seawater crevasse? My body, wrapped in a life vest, would fall into the gap, then be crushed as a wave pushed the two ships together.

My turn came. I poised myself, feet planted on the gunnel. I looked down on the faces of the men standing on the launch's bobbling deck.

"Jump," they shouted over the wind's howl. "Jump!" I paused, thinking of what might happen if I missed. My legs and hips landed hard on the deck of the launch, but there was no escaping the terrifying image that preceded my jump. For sixty-five years, from time to time, the nightmare has haunted my sleep.

As for the *Lamorna*, mastless and abandoned in the windswept Channel, she continued her westward drift, avoiding the stranding on the Needles that had been feared. The fierce gale had caused the skippers of other ships in the Channel to issue calls for rescue. The tide was running against the wind, making the sea even rougher. To

Top: the 140-foot schooner Lamorna. *Bottom Left: the destroyer* Redpole *fails in her first attempt to shoot a towline to the crippled* Lamorna. *Bottom Right: crew members salvage belongings from the mastless* Lamorna *after the storm.*

the west of us off the Cornish coast, a small Spanish steamer with seventeen men on board ran onto Black Rock Head, pounded on the reef for several minutes, was washed off, and blown northeastwards. The collision with the rock had punched a hole in the hull, and the ship was filling with water. When a lifeboat arrived, the ship was only fifty yards off the rocks where the sea was breaking heavily. The lifeboat's coxswain saw that in a few minutes she would be on them. He must act at once. In a daring maneuver, he took the lifeboat in towards the rocks, then back out again to the foundering ship. The waves were already breaking over her. The coxswain called on the crew to jump. One hesitated, then jumped, and soon the other sixteen men followed, landing safely on the rescue boat's deck. The departed wreck later washed ashore.

About the same time, a steamship with forty aboard had broken down and was being dragged towards Black Rock. A rescue boat saved her, but only after the tow rope broke off several times. To the north, an Italian steamer, with a cargo of iron ore, signaled that the gale and rough sea was pushing her towards rocks and needed towing. A rescue boat saved her.

Our own rescue launch bore us to Yarmouth harbor on the Isle of Wight, where we spent the night. The next day Ian Rogers, Geoff Taylor, and I took the ferry to the mainland, and rented a taxi to take us to a gravel beach not far from Bournemouth. There we found the wrecked hull of the *Lamorna*. Making our way through a tangle of mast and rigging, we were able to descend into the cabin and retrieve our belongings.

Two months later, the following report appeared in the Yarmouth news section of the *Isle of Wight Press*: "The gallant rescue of fourteen from the ill-fated treasure ship *Lamorna* off the Needles on November 4th, was recalled when the crew of the lifeboat were entertained at dinner on board the navigation instructional ship *HMS Redpole*. Although cooperating closely in the rescue work, the crews of the two vessels had previously seen one another only in the glare of searchlights, and their only communication had been by radio-telephone."

Captain Kidd's own real treasure was later said to have been buried on Providenciales Island in the Turks and Caicos in the Atlantic, north of Haiti. An inlet and small peninsula on Providenciales look remarkably like the shape of the island on our treasure map. The Marquis had missed spotting it. Possibly Kidd briefly buried his treasure there, then removed it. In 1976 a group of men hacked their way through dense underbrush, and uncovered a location where something had been buried, a feat I was unable to duplicate in 1995 when I visited Providenciales.

To where Kidd's treasure went no one has ever firmly discovered.

After the escape from drowning in the English Channel, I worked my way home on a freighter crossing the North Atlantic in the winter of 1952. In Montreal I found a job writing press releases and editing corporate sales and employee magazines. I married my college sweet-heart, who'd awaited my return from Europe, and was working as a reporter at the *Montreal Gazette* daily newspaper. We had two children. We divorced after five years of marriage. She moved with the children to her native Vermont.

I departed for New York City.

CHAPTER 6

DEATH BY THE NUMBERS

World Death Rate Holds Steady at 100%.

The Onion, January 22, 1997

Three weeks after emigrating from Canada to the U.S. in 1957, I found a job at a daily newspaper just north of Wall Street in Manhattan's financial district. *American Metal Market* was located on Cliff Street, a short narrow lane that no longer exists. A four-story brick building housed the printing press, shipping, and linotype machines at street level, a floor of desks where the editors worked, and the offices of the advertising staff and the publisher on the top floor. If an easterly wind were blowing, the odor of fresh halibut and cod occasionally wafted into the offices from the Fulton Fish Market, a block away.

At my desk, on a Remington upright typewriter, I hammered out a daily department, feature articles, and editorials about the economic impact of brass mill shutdowns in Connecticut, the outlook for zinc, whether Kennecott would raise the price of copper, labor strife among miners in Chile and Africa's Katanga. I traveled to Brussels to interview officials at the three-year-old European Common Market, and to London to learn the mysteries of London Metal Exchange trading.

The newspaper's pages were chockablock with numbers—the quotidian prices of steel and nonferrous scrap, indices of production, volume of consumption. Out of the experience came knowledge about statistics and an intense interest in them that occupies a twisted amount of space in my mind to this day, sometimes irksome to those otherwise nearest and dearest to me.

With statistics you can always find a number at odds with another. If one statistic radiates pessimism, another can be found bathed in optimism. For example, in his remarkable and wonderfully readable book *Sapiens*, Yuval Noah Harari proves statistically how much less violent the world is today compared with how it was a thousand years ago. How can that be when we daily watch on TV and read about so much mayhem and violence in today's world? "

Harari explains. When the world population was 320 million, around the time of medieval Europe, about twenty to forty people were murdered each year for every 100,000 inhabitants. Today, with a world population of 7.7 billion, the average is only nine murders per 100,000. The year 2000 witnessed the tragic deaths of 830,000 men, women and children. "Yet from a macro perspective," writes Harari, these 830,000 victims comprised only 1.5 percent of the fifty-six million people who died, a far lower percentage than a thousand years ago. Statistically we are safer. Go figure.

The statistic of most intense interest to all of us, of course, is how long we'll get to live. If you're a woman you can expect to live five years longer than a man. The average American woman in 2018 died at age 81.2 years, a man at 76.1.

Senescence is a time of weakening defenses against infection, pneumonia, stroke, fractures from falls, the dangers in surgery. Arteries narrow, lessening the supply of oxygen and nutrients to vital body regions. Sensory and motor nerves sputter. The incidence of Parkinson's and dementia has doubled statistically in the twenty-first century. Alzheimer's has become the fifth leading cause of death of people over 65 years of age, and there's no medicine for it. At the same time modern medicine has driven people to live longer. At age 90 I've gone past the age when, by mathematical average calculation, I was supposed to die. I've broken through the statistical boundary.

As we advance in age, the older we'll be when we die. In 1935 an average 65-year-old person could expect to live another 12 years, reaching age 77. Today if we reach the age of 65, statistically we can expect to live another 20 years to age 85. At age 90, actuarial tables give me another four years to live. As I write this, I ask myself if I will have enough time to see this book published.

Today's older men and women—baby boomers who emerged from the womb in the years 1944 to 1964—live longer than people did when they were born. But they've now reached the age of dying themselves. Sixty million baby boomers will die between 2020 and 2050. On average now, 4,750 die daily.

Notwithstanding this bulge of older people in the population, the average U.S. life span has actually been declining since the beginning of the twenty-first century. Adults between the ages of twenty-five and sixty-four, especially white people in Midwestern states like Ohio, Pennsylvania, and Indiana affected by industry closures, are dying earlier. Deaths involving fentanyl have increased by more than forty-five percent.

Perhaps the biggest factor contributing to the statistical life-span decline, though, is the rising number of young persons dying earlier. Drug overdoses, accidents, and suicides are behind the soaring mortality rate of people between twenty-four and forty-four years of age. More people are doing themselves in. Suicide is second only to accidents as the cause of death among ten- to twenty-four-year-olds.

The rapid rise in attempted and completed suicide among teenagers correlates directly with their access to cellphones and the internet. Young brains aren't especially adept at dealing with social complexity, which has been altered and amplified by the technology behind social media. The new complexity may not be well understood, but the statistic is clear, a deathly warning to parents.

Between 2000 and 2018 the overall suicide rate in America doubled to 45,000 annually. This figure of 45,000 happens to be the same as the number of veterans and active-duty service members who committed suicide during the six years leading up to 2019, according to *The New York Times*. In other words, the statistical population of military suffering PTSD and other depressive impacts of warfare now accounts for roughly a sixth of all American suicides.

The poor live shorter lives, too. Of Americans born in the ten years after I was born in 1930, only half of those in the bottom twenty percent of wage earners were still alive in 2014. Among people whose incomes were in the top twenty percent, by contrast, three out of four were still alive. I don't know what income percentile I belong to, but clearly I've made enough money to enable me to celebrate my ninetieth birthday.

With the exception of older people covered by Medicare, people under the age of sixty-five, suffering from illnesses like type 2 diabetes, disabling joint pain, and severe infections, don't have free access to universal health care in a country whose per capita health-care cost is the highest in the world.

On the brighter side, the average dying age of black men has risen almost to the level of white men, 76.2 years; in 1993 an African American man's life was 8.5 years shorter.

A life expectancy statistic can be a risky gamble. Famous is the story of the French lawyer who agreed to pay a ninety-year-old woman 2,500 francs per month until she died, whereupon he would come to own her apartment. Statistically he was counting on her dying in just a few years' time. Who wouldn't? But the woman didn't die. She lived to the remarkable, unprecedented age of one hundred twenty-two, outliving the lawyer who died at age seventy-seven.

Because of my interest in environmental protection (I served on the boards of the Pinchot Institute for Conservation and of Riverkeeper, battling polluters of the Hudson River), one statistic that I regard as noxious is that purporting to gauge the nation's progress. Gross national product (GNP) or gross domestic product (GDP) measures production of material things, not advances in people's health or happiness. Politicians trumpet rising GDP as a sign of their policy successes; falling GDP leads to their not being reelected. It may also be observed that a society defining its progress in this manner unfortunately produces many people who value their existence in the same way.

Imagine believing that a rise in your body's temperature, measured by a thermometer, is an indication of good health. Obviously, it's not. It leads to sickness. Yet the more a country's GNP or GDP rises, the better off we're assumed to be.

The largest component of GDP is the use of products like automobiles, TVs, armaments, planes, plastics, heating, air-conditioning and more—products whose manufacture adds to atmospheric carbon and ozone loss. Carbon dioxide, because of its molecular structure, traps heat in the atmosphere. More than half of the CO_2 exhaled into the atmosphere by the burning of fossil fuels was emitted in the thirty years between 1997 and 2017.

Unmeasured in GNP or GDP are immense losses from deforestation, disappearing agriculture and wetlands, methane emitted from thawing permafrost, and the migrations of people seeking to escape rising seawater levels, mudslides, heat, and starvation. Worldwide, in 2018 extreme weather events displaced a record seven million people from their homes.

So it is that GDP and GNP contribute to millions of people dying from starvation, drowning, air and water poisoning, wind blasting, heat prostration. Yet these indices crudely and unreasonably measure the health of almost all national economies.

My career as a journalist has coincided with a rise in statistical illiteracy: reporters unable to parse numbers well, organizations that don't understand their own statistics correctly or misuse words. Some of the loss is in language. Latin—which I studied as a schoolboy, and which earned me a McGill University scholarship—is no longer taught. In the inevitable swamp of ensuing linguistic ignorance, data and media—Latin plural words—have become singular. Radio, now a media, was once a medium among the media of television, magazines, and movies. Data no longer inform us, it informs us. So it's not surprising that data or facts get screwed up too.

As an example, the U.S. Open Tennis Center in 2019 boasted that 737,872 fans attended the matches. In fact, it sold 737,872 tickets, many of them to the same fans. So it's likely that maybe half as many people attended the matches, not 737,872.

During a given winter, U.S. ski areas experience around 55 million visits. The actual number of skiers and snowboarders, however, is only roughly known. That did not discourage the ski industry's two leading trade organizations from issuing participant numbers five million apart. The odds of dying from a skiing accident, by the way, are slim— less than one per one million visits. Bicycling may be more dangerous.

Only a few months after I'd landed the editorial job at *American Metal Market* I spotted an ad in the employment classified section of *The New York Times*. It was from a publisher seeking an editor for a new national magazine for skiers, called *Ski Life*. I'd ski-raced in college, so I went for an interview with the publisher, Arnold Abramson, who the year before had launched *Golf* magazine. He immediately wanted to hire me.

"Wow!" I thought to myself. "This new job is going to be singularly better than riding the subway train down to Wall Street every day, editing stories on the impact of tariffs on aluminum imports."

Aware of my penchant for foolish schemes, I took the precaution of asking, "What's the salary?"

"Five thousand dollars," Abramson replied. It was a third less than what I was making at *American Metal Market*, far short of the money I needed to support an ex-wife and two young children who were living in Stowe, Vermont.

The experience, it turned out, was similar to one I would have two years later. At an aluminum industry press conference in 1960, I met John Lee who was covering the metals beat for *The New York Times*.

"I'm getting a promotion," Lee told me. "My present job as a Business Section reporter at the *Times* is open. I'm sure if you apply, you'll get it."

Wow! Working for the prestigious *New York Times* would be a real upgrade, singularly better than an editorial job at a small-circulation trade daily.

"What's the salary?"

"Maybe $5,000."

"Is that all the *Times* pays, John? I have two kids to support. I can't afford it." (Lee would go on to become assistant managing editor of the *Times*. Thirty-eight years later we laughed when I finally became a fellow Times Company employee and editor. We remained close friends until the day he died in 2009.)

In conclusion, I agreed to do freelance writing and editing for the new ski magazine. Five years later, after the publisher bought and merged it into *Ski*—America's oldest and largest-circulation magazine for skiers—he hired me.

CHAPTER 7

LIVING AND DYING IN PRINT

The 1920s to the 2020s was kind of the century of the magazine. Today the industry is in more of a slow dusk, and we're closer to sunset. Magazines may eventually gain a cult following akin to obsolete media, like vinyl records. Eventually they'll become like sailboats. They don't need to exist anymore. But people will still love them, and make them and buy them.

Kurt Andersen, a former editor of *New York* and a founder of *Spy* magazine, as reported in *The New York Times*, September 23, 2017

I was born to work in an industry—the printed magazine—that was robust and healthy when I entered it in the middle of the twentieth century. By the twenty-first it was experiencing a deathly illness.

The desire to edit was deeply rooted in me, like an inherited metabolism. When I was nine years old I published a weekly one-page account of news on our street, printed on a borrowed mimeograph machine. As a teenager, I was a reporter for a citywide high-school newspaper. In college, I edited the campus humor magazine.

Now I'd just departed my job as managing editor of a daily business paper. As *Ski*'s new editor in chief in 1964, I enjoyed a corner window office on Second Avenue and Forty-second Street, diagonally across from the *New York Daily News* building. After pencil editing, manuscripts were retyped, then dispatched to the printer, where a linotype machine operator keyed the copy in again. From the typesetter came galley proofs, which were carefully read, corrections penciled. The columns of galley type were pasted into page layouts. The pleasant smell of rubber cement radiated from the art department. That long-ago era of publishing, now dead, lingers in my memory as the taste and smell of madeleines did for Proust.

With the job came expense-paid trips to any snow-covered mountain in the world. Over the next five years, I traveled to Russia's Caucasus Mountains, the Atlas Mountains of Morocco, the French Alps, and in British Columbia when the Bugaboo Lodge first opened for helicopter skiing. I skied the trails of at least two dozen resorts from Maine to California, and was with my friend Johannes von Trapp in 1968 when he opened America's first commercial cross-country ski-touring center.

In 1969 I became editorial director of the monthly *Golf* as well as of *Ski*, whose seven issues were published between September and March. The magazine industry was thriving. It was a golden age. Tens of millions of readers subscribed to *Life, Look, Time, Ladies' Home Journal,* or purchased these magazines at newsstands. *Reader's Digest* alone had a paid circulation of eighteen million. Special-interest magazines—about automobiles, boating, cooking, carpentry, flying, music, skiing and golf—were doubling their circulation numbers.

But the year 1969 contained the first hint of vulnerability, with the shutdown of *The Saturday Evening Post*. A few years later, *Life, Look,* and others ceased publication. They were hurt by the soaring circulation and advertising success of the sort of special-interest magazines where I was working. The greater destruction, though, came from television. Now in color and seen on ever-larger screens, TV lured armchair sitters from reading to viewing and hearing.

A day has only twenty-four hours. Most of the hours are spent working, sleeping, eating, commuting, housekeeping, and other necessary activities. What's left is discretionary time, much of it devoted to absorbing information and entertainment on a TV screen or a computer monitor.

Given a fixed amount of time, when one medium grows in size, there is less time for another. One medium cedes its superiority, or its location, to another medium. Radio listening moved out of the home to the car. More TV watching led to less reading of books and magazines. More time engaged in social media on the internet would eventually lead to less time spent watching conventional television, and even less for reading magazines. Though none entirely dies, media are in constant war with one another to capture our time.

In 1984, after I left Times Mirror Magazines where I'd been editorial director, I wrote a column on magazine editing for *Folio*, the magazine of magazine management, and achieved some success as a magazine startup consultant. In 1987 the New York Times Company retained me to create a new magazine for skiers. *Snow Country* received a 1992 Acres of Diamonds Award as one of America's thirteen best new magazines.

While at the Times Co., I briefly headed a group looking into magazine development. An oxymoron. The futility of the work in retrospect was rather colossal . . . like studying the market potential for dictionaries in a country largely populated by illiterates.

While television and the internet are blamed for the downfall of magazines, some of the suffering experienced by publishers was self-inflicted. Where to begin?

Henry Luce once built his Time Life magazine empire on the premise of hiring brilliant editors, writers, and photographers to attract readers. With enough readers, Luce believed, he could attract advertisers. By the 1980s, though, Luce's dictum had been turned on its head. A magazine came into existence if it could attract advertisers sufficiently so that it was worthwhile for the publisher to seek desperately for people to read it. *Ski* magazine, for example, wound up giving away two-thirds of its subscriptions in a manner known as free controlled circulation. Editorial departments were created at magazines not to supply subject matter especially attractive to readers, but to supply subject matter attractive to advertisers.

Publishers gradually lost faith in strong editors to shape their magazines. At the top of the masthead of more than one magazine, above the name of the editor was that of the Creative Director, presumably there because the publisher regarded his editor as lacking in creativity—the very quality, along with curiosity, that should have been the reason for hiring the editor in the first place.

With some magazines the title of Editor has disappeared entirely from mastheads, replaced by Content Director, a person whose job primarily calls for trafficking subject matter among print, online, blogs, podcasts, and social media like Facebook.

Publishers came to provide much of their print content free at a website. In most cases, however, website advertising failed to compensate publishers for the print revenue they'd lost, not only from advertisers who migrated to Google, but also from readers no longer willing to pay for content that had been made available free on the websites publishers themselves had created.

As Kurt Andersen suggests at the beginning of this chapter, print magazines that do not die may be kept alive with the help of charitable giving, just as community movie theaters are being kept alive. I'm the chairperson of a nonprofit association that raises $150,000 a year in donations to publish a print bimonthly, *Skiing History*. Only a fraction of our costs are borne by subscribers. More than four hundred individuals and fifty corporate sponsors supply the rest.

Among the magazines I edited in the 1970s was *Outdoor Life*. Founded in 1898, and one of America's oldest continuously published magazines, it was a monthly read by more than a million-and-a-half hunters and fishermen. Hunting was on the decline when I became editorial director in 1976, so I proposed to the publisher that we begin to devote fewer pages to killing animals, and more to their natural histories. The magazine's subscription renewal rate rose in response. But I ultimately failed. The publisher feared firearm companies like Remington and Winchester, advertisers in *Outdoor Life*, would not like a retreat from traditional hook-and-bullet content. After I left Times Mirror, bigger editorial problems arose when the National Rifle Association switched from a hunting-oriented organization to a politically oriented organization focused on the right to bear arms and defending the notion that gun owners should be able to add high-capacity magazines of the kind used in assault weapons to kill people in warfare. With more and more sophisticated rifles and ammo, the challenges and ethics of hunting declined, as did the number of hunters, as I'd predicted.

No longer a monthly, *Outdoor Life* is now issued only quarterly, and it has less than a half-million subscribers. Never gone from its pages, though, are the stories of bear attacks, beloved by readers.

CHAPTER 8

DEATH BY BEAR ATTACK

He climbed the nearest tree and wasn't too worried for he knew he would be safe, as grizzly bears don't climb trees. He was nearly ten feet up the tree before he looked down. He was terrified when he saw the snarling grizzly scrambling after him and climbing fast. He felt the bear grab his leg and its teeth tore his skin and muscle. The bear fell but quickly climbed again and this time his teeth bit hard into his thigh. The man was so frightened he didn't feel any pain.

Ben East, *Danger!*

As noted earlier, I once worked as the editorial director of one of America's oldest continuously published magazines, *Outdoor Life*, its pages read by hunters and fishermen for over a hundred and twenty years. For the magazine's million-and-a-half subscribers, no stories were more beloved than the thrillers about the unfortunate man or woman, out in the woods for a walk, who is viciously attacked by a bear, preferably a grizzly, or an angry mother brown bear protecting her cubs.

As told by the victim, his clothes and skin are savagely shredded. The bear grabs his leg with its mouth, sinking its fangs into his flesh. From the pocket of his parka he either pulls out a can of pepper spray or a loaded Ruger revolver and fires it at the bear who yowls in agony and retreats into the bush.

Few die in the bear attack stories. The terrified and injured remain alive for the benefit of freelance writers and the publishers who pay them for their as-told-to stories. The language of the bear attack was vivid, spine-tingling to readers. *Outdoor* writers sloshed around in gory words.

> *The bear came at me ... with ears flattened, neck hairs stiffly erect, it growled fiercely as it charged full bore at me. I saw its flashing teeth as it came.*

> *Eyes blazing, and swinging his great blocky head from side to side, he lunged from the bush with a low growl.*

The master of this genre of storytelling was Ben East, author of two dozen adventure books crammed with bloodcurdling human-bear encounters. I once flew to Wisconsin to spend a couple of days with East learning his craft, and how I could exploit it to spur the magazine's single-copy sales and subscription renewals.

Years later I found myself in a setting often described by East, alone in the wilderness. In celebration of my sixtieth birthday I'd decided to make a solo climb of Mount Marcy, New York state's highest mountain. It was Columbus Day weekend. The sky was cloudless, the sun warmed the crisp mountain air. My plan was not to go up Marcy's 3,200 vertical feet from the base, a seven-mile rise over mud and rock, in a single day. Rather I'd accomplish it in two stages, camping overnight, halfway up at Indian Falls.

Twenty years earlier, my son and I had spent a winter night at the falls in one of the lean-to shelters. The shelters had since been torn down. The former campground was now home to whitetail deer, raccoons, the odd marten, bobcat, coyote, and porcupine. Unknown to me, it had also become prime black bear habitat.

Reaching Indian Falls at dusk, I placed my sleeping bag on the open ground and ate a sandwich that I'd packed. On the low-hanging branch of a spruce, I hung my boots and the rucksack containing dehydrated food, figs, and a chocolate bar. The night was uncommonly warm for October and the ground all around was illuminated by a full moon.

At two in the morning a noise near my head awakened me. It sounded like the grunting of a pig, and came from the base of the tree where I'd hung the pack. It took me about a minute before I realized that the noise was coming from a bear, maybe within a dozen feet of where I was lying.

Carefully, gingerly, I slipped out of the sleeping bag and walked away, barefoot on the wet ground. I had enough presence of mind to grab my parka and my socks to bring with me. After walking about fifty feet, I stopped and shone my flashlight back at where the animal was probably foraging through my belongings. When I made a noise and tried to return, it snorted ominously. So I barefooted my way along the trail to an open ledge above Indian Falls.

I put on my socks, and waited. Ten minutes later, illuminated by the moon, the bear appeared nightmarishly on the open rock. It passed about a dozen yards away from where I was sitting. I watched it drink from the stream, and heard it burp with satisfaction from swallowing whatever food I imagined it had ransacked from my pack. I was alone and terrified. No one was within miles of where I was. Did the bear suspect that I was carrying food that it would want to eat?

"This guy will follow me all night," I thought. I spotted a tall spruce with branches so dense that I imagined a bear would be unlikely to climb it.

I sprinted to the base of the tree and jammed my body upward through its branches. As I climbed, my hair filled with needles, my hands became sticky with spruce gum. Fifteen feet up, I found a perch. Thighs resting on a couple of branches, I opened the brass closure on my belt. It was long enough so that I could wrap the leather strap around the tree's trunk. If I were to fall asleep, the belt, attached to my waist, would prevent me from falling out of the tree, maybe onto the bear waiting at the base. I would wait for the sun to come up in the morning.

The bear almost surely has followed me, I thought. Frightening was the anticipation that the beast might attempt to climb through the dense growth to where I was sitting. I imagined how the animal would use its powerful jaws and teeth to grab my feet and pull me down. I would topple to the ground where he'd tear at my clothing and flesh. Into my mind came the words of my friend and neighbor Chris Davis in a story that he wrote in the *Reader's Digest* about a 2007 grizzly attack on a young Canadian man trapped under a tree.

> *When he looked out, the bear was about 30 centimeters from his face, mouth wide, teeth and gums exposed, pointing its nose up to make the coughing, humphing sound of territorial aggression. With his right hand, Jeff poked at his predator's eyes. But the bear took Jeff's hand in its mouth, fangs sinking deep into his flesh, then spit it out.*

Visions crossed my mind of what might happen. First there'd be the excruciating pain of the animal's claws ripping my skin. Then the teeth pulling at a chunk of my flesh. My blood pressure would sink as I passed into unconsciousness.

In the tree I slipped in and out of sleep. My head was resting on a fragrant branch of needles that served as a pillow. At six o'clock in the morning the dawn light glowed brightly enough so that I could see there was no bear at the foot of the tree. I detached my belt from the trunk, and forced my way down through the thicket of branches. As I neared the ground, I could see paw marks around the tree's base.

I walked back to where I'd camped and found my sleeping bag

untouched. My boots were still slung over the tree, and I put them on. At first I didn't see my rucksack. Then I spotted it twenty feet away in a thick stand of spruce. I walked over to it and saw the nylon sack had been torn to shreds. Inside it, the only food the bear had found to his taste was a chocolate bar.

I was more than halfway up Mount Marcy, and determined still to complete the climb to the summit. On an empty stomach, in the rain, I slogged my way upward through the fog. The rain pelted horizontally out of the sky. The wind scoured my face. It would have been easy to turn back, abandon another foolish scheme, but in my addled mind retreat would've been defeat.

I knew I'd hit the summit when I caught sight of the moss-covered rock bearing the bronze plaque recording Marcy's history. After spending a couple of minutes reading that the Indian name for the mountain is Tahawus, and that 5,344-foot Mount Marcy was first climbed in 1837, I turned around and headed back down the trail to my car, passing Indian Falls and the home of the harmless bear. Perhaps it was watching me, snorting with amusement.

After four hours I reached the bottom, exhausted. My feet were blistered, blood oozed from under the nail of a big toe. Yet I was surprised by the reserves of stamina and resolve left in me after sixty years. I was happy to have deferred old age for a while.

CHAPTER 9

COURTING DEATH

"Because it's there."

George Leigh Mallory, on being asked
why he wanted to climb Mount Everest. He died doing it.

It was once like this: people set out to go from point A to point B because it hadn't been done. The adventure amplified if they drowned, accidentally fell into a crevasse or down an escarpment during a whiteout, or got caught in an avalanche. Mortal risk was a byproduct of going faster, reaching a higher place.

Advances in equipment and clothing, communication, global positioning, and helicopter rescue have made once-extreme goals easier to attain. The North Pole has been reached, Everest climbed, Antarctica crossed. If every mountain has been climbed, every river's source reached, every patch of the world explored, the only solution is to find more and more difficult ways to do the same. In order to intensify the challenge, routes have been made more complex and difficult. In rock climbing, skiing, rafting, and skydiving, extremity became the new norm.

For readers I published numerous adventure stories about men and women making first ski descents of the world's highest mountains, breaking speed records, and exploring remote regions of hostile climate and terrain. A Norwegian replicated Fritdjof Nansen's 1888 feat of crossing Greenland on skis, cannibalizing his dogs to survive. I featured a story about Ned Gillette and Jan Reynolds making a successful descent on skis of 24,547-foot Mustagh Ata in western China, at the time the highest mountain ever skied from its summit, an exploit that came about as a result of contacts made when I traveled with them to the former Manchuria in 1980, cross-country skiing.

In the distant past of 1938, when I was eight, Englishman George Leigh Mallory struggled to be the first man to reach the summit of Everest, falling and dying in the descent. By the time I was eighty years old, the deadliest risk on the world's highest mountain was becoming trapped in a horde of inexperienced climbers, with their guides jammed together like frantic commuters simultaneously trying to enter and exit an overfilled subway car.

The granddaddy of risk is the north side of Switzerland's Eiger peak, known as the Death Wall. During my lifetime almost seventy climbers have met gruesome ends on the Eiger's north face, leaving in their wake dozens of widows and fatherless children.

In America, no longer is it sufficient to scale Yosemite's El Capitan. The climber free-solos it without rope or belay, filmed so that millions of us can see a man taunting the Grim Reaper. One failed grip or foothold and Alex Honnold would have plunged to his death, making *Free Solo*, to say the least, a radically different kind of movie.

Lover of risk, Ned Gillette determined in 1988 to do a voyage something like the one experienced by Ernest Shackleton when he had attempted to cross Antarctica from sea to sea in 1915, and failed. To escape, Shackleton and his crew nearly perished, drifting and rowing northeast from Antarctica.

For his voyage, Gillette, with three other men, would row a boat from the southwestern tip of Chile to Antarctica, eight hundred miles across the world's most violent, treacherous waters. If they were blown off course, their lives were at risk. Fatal would be a collision with an iceberg.

For his crazy, death-defying voyage, Gillette, at forty-two, built an unsinkable boat he called *Sea Tomato*. He and his crew rowed in shifts, battered by wind, towering waves, penetrating wet cold. If a wave capsized the *Sea Tomato*, she righted herself. When one wave did just that, Gillette was thrown into the sea, saved from drowning because he was lashed to the boat by lifeline. After thirteen days, *Sea Tomato* and her crew reached the South Shetland Islands off the coast of Antarctica.

"What did we accomplish?" asked Gillette in an article he wrote for *National Geographic*. "Nothing of great benefit to mankind perhaps, other than a daring challenge met and conquered. The greater achievement was the inner voyage."

Gillette, who pioneered ways to inveigle sponsors to fund his trips and who was killed by robbers in Pakistan in 1998, was on the cutting edge of the transformation in adventure.

Early in the twenty-first century a weirder zeitgeist appeared. Instead of accidentally getting caught in an avalanche and hopefully surviving, testosterone-charged men began the game of deliberately inserting themselves in an avalanche. In a sport called "high-marking," snowmobilers ride as high as possible on a slope, then surf down a snow slide they've triggered. An avalanche is not something to avoid; you're a chicken if you don't outrace one.

"We've got people actually trying to cause avalanches," says Bruce Tremper, who heads the Utah Avalanche Center. "It's a sport." Journalist Tim Egan called it "the intersection of risk and stupidity." In the ten years leading to 2018, two hundred and fifty-nine avalanche fatalities were recorded; half maybe were of snowboarders and snow-mobilers. Kids on boards plunge down narrow chutes, lined with rocks, simulating the stars in extreme-sport videos. The most neglectful don't wear head protection.

Here is the arrogance of risk: I can do whatever I want. I can ski without a helmet or in a forest riddled with tree wells, or at a time when avalanche warnings have been posted, simply because I dare to. After all, I'm not holding others responsible for what happens. Not true. There is the selfishness of disregarding the danger to volunteers who may have to rescue the adventurer, and the absence of empathy felt for immediate family who suffer and grieve over the deaths or near-fatal injuries.

"Why not just to leave it up to people's own choice?" asked Owen, a youthful extreme skier whom I encountered at one website and who proved to be a microcosm of what has gone haywire. "Hell, if they get caught, it's there (sic) problem."

Hello out there, Mom and Dad, have you talked recently with your Owen?

Seeking to build commerce with the Owens of the world, commercial streaming, videos, and specialized outdoor magazines celebrate the glory of the extreme. They glamorize precipitous descents of hazardous, rock-strewn slopes.

"On the edge for you is the middle of the road for me," read one braggart's bumper sticker. Mountain Dew, the soft drink, once sought to overcome its own insipidity by linking its image to awesome feats.

My friend, Canadian-born Jim McConkey, himself once an extreme skier (Chapter 4), pleaded with his son Shane McConkey to halt his prodigious risk-taking after he married and had a child. On March 26, 2009, Shane skied off a precipice in the Italian Dolomites, wearing a body suit with wings that enabled him to fly like a bird. Once separated from the cliff and in mid-air, he was unable to detach his

skis and deploy his parachute. Within a few seconds he plunged verti-
cally to his death. He was thirty-nine. Shane died a hero to thousands of
young men who venture into the backcountry, echoing his ideal.

To pursue risk for risk's sake, admittedly, is to go against a boring,
convention-ridden society overly concerned with safety. In 1968 I
traveled to British Columbia's mountains where I experienced and
wrote about the first helicopter-assisted skiing out of the new
Bugaboo Lodge, where Geoffrey Taylor later became the first recreational skier to die heli-skiing (Chapter 4). In the following twenty
years, thirty more Canadian Mountain Holidays skiers would die in
tree wells and in avalanches similar to the one that killed my friend.
They were on vacation.

Risk-taking is typically a byproduct of wanting to prove one's
superiority within a peer group. Risk rises with the human inclina-
tion to do what everyone seems to be doing, or experts say it's okay.
Matters become potentially fatal, as one climbs higher or goes deeper,
and turning around, going back, becomes increasingly difficult, then
impossible, perhaps a metaphor for life itself.

Is the urge to surpass others justified by the consequence?
Justified, or tragic, in whose mind? Sacrificed for what? When I was
nearly finished writing this book, I learned that one of the world's
most important theoretical physicists, Steven Gubser, at forty-seven
had fallen to his death while climbing a dangerous rock needle next
to Mont Blanc. Gubser was a keen, skilled climber. A string theorist,

he may have been close to achieving the long-dreamt-of reconciliation of the differences separating General Relativity from subatomic particle theory, the famous "explanation of everything."

The world was deprived of the secret of its existence because its potential discoverer chose the thrill of risking death. Or maybe God arranged that Gubser die because He didn't want His secret revealed.

CHAPTER 10

SUICIDE

It would be ridiculous that a man should spend his life in a way that brought him as near as possible to being dead, then complain of death when it came.

Socrates in *Phaedo*, prior to his committing suicide with hemlock poison

You say that those who threaten or hint suicide won't do it. We suspect that this is not so. Many suicides talk about it for a good time before, as many doctors have discovered to their chagrin.

Letter from Humphry Osmond to Aldous Huxley, November 25, 1956

"**H**umphry, on this chart of a schizophrenic you write that he's 'a successful suicide.' The wording seems unfeeling, heartless."

"Well, the patient successfully performed the act," replied Humphry Osmond, addressing me in his high-pitched voice, his accent unaffected by his migration from London to North America eighteen years earlier. "After all, the man succeeded at what he wanted to do."

The year was 1969. I had a full-time job as editorial director of *Ski* and *Golf* magazines. In the evenings and on weekends I was editing the manuscript of a soon-to-be-published book and test, *The Experiential World Inventory*. The EWI was a revolutionary way to diagnose mental illness. Humphry Osmond, its coauthor, was the psychiatrist noted for guiding the writer Aldous Huxley through his initial experiences with psychedelics—mescalin and LSD (lysergic acid diethylamide)—inspiring Huxley to write his bestselling *Doors of Perception*.

The two Englishmen, both born in Surrey, were transplanted to geographic opposites—Huxley to sun-warmed, star-studded Hollywood, Osmond to the frigid, lonely prairie of Saskatchewan. Between these strangely disparate points they wrote to one another, sometimes weekly. Their correspondence is crammed with remarkable insights and criticisms, especially ideas on how society's ills could be cured through the use of hallucinogens. The men ardently believed that if political, industrial, educational, and religious leaders could be persuaded to experience the effects of mescalin and LSD, it would open their minds to a transcendent world they would otherwise never know, and society would be transformed. These remarkable letters, written by the two intellectuals between 1952 and 1962, are contained in the book *Psychedelic Prophets* published in 2018. I happily attended the book's publication party at the Morgan Library in New York.

In the letters, and in countless papers and talks, Osmond argued that LSD showed promise in psychotherapy, with a particularly encouraging potential for curing alcoholism. Not surprisingly, he was bitterly disappointed when LSD, popularized by Timothy Leary and Ken Kesey, became not the marvelous curative he dreamed of, but rather a recreational drug for rebellious young people, leading to its criminalization. The drug's disrepute endured for almost seventy years, Osmond's belief in its therapeutic value ignored or forgotten. Finally, in 2019, the Johns Hopkins Center for Psychedelic and Consciousness Research and Imperial College in England announced that they had raised upwards of $20 million to evaluate the use of LSD and psilocybin in addressing mental-health problems—exactly what Osmond was trying to do back in the 1950s!

Before I met Osmond, he had been the head of the rundown Weyburn mental hospital in southern Saskatchewan. There he and his colleague, Abe Hoffer, a Canadian biochemist and psychiatrist, had devised a novel test for evaluating the hospital's nearly one thousand patients. The Hoffer Osmond Diagnostic Test (HOD) differed from verbal tests predominantly used in psychological diagnosis, particularly the Minnesota Multiphasic Personality Inventory.

The HOD was a tool to determine, first, whether the person being examined was schizophrenic, and second, whether the illness was deeply depressive or paranoid, and if it might have a potential for suicide. The HOD questionnaire was built on a vocabulary not of normal people but of already mentally ill people. It measured not deviations from normal, but rather alignment with the abnormal. The test was rooted in the language of the mentally ill patients whom Osborn and Hoffer observed at the Weyburn hospital.

When I look at things like tables and chairs they seem strange.

I have heard voices coming from the radio, television, or tape recorders talking about me.

There are people trying to do me harm.

I feel as if I am dead.

I find that past, present, and future seem all muddled up.

The more the patient agreed with such statements, the more severe his mental illness. The HOD was a diagnostic tool, which Osmond saw as superior to the obscure, recondite interpretations of Rorschach inkblots and Freudian psychology. He had an especially low regard for Freudian analysis in diagnosing mental illness, thinking it close to useless.

The problem with the HOD test, however, was that it was weak in measurable reliability and validity, making it unacceptable for broader use in professional psychiatry. The solution came to Osmond after he left Saskatchewan and moved to Princeton, where he became director of the Bureau of Research in Neurology and Psychiatry at the New Jersey Psychiatric Institute. In Princeton he met Moneim El-Meligi, an Egyptian and a first-rate psychologist. The two men collaborated in doing the necessary psychometric studies missing in the HOD. They amended and expanded the questionnaire, giving it a new name: "Experiential World Inventory." With its greatly expanded vocabulary, the EWI better identified varieties of schizophrenia, enabling clinicians to determine what therapy and medications to employ.

But who would finance the EWI's publication and use? Osmond earlier had been in touch with wealthy Toronto venture capitalist Ben Webster, who had used LSD under his monitoring. Webster fervently endorsed the idea that the doors of perception opened by mescalin and LSD had the potential to improve the world. Would Webster, asked Osmond, be willing to fund the publication and distribution of the EWI? Yes, came the answer. But how? Webster informed Osmond and El-Meligi that his lifelong friend John Fry, a publishing professional in New York, would arrange for the EWI's publication. And so I did.

Osmond came to lunch at our Manhattan brownstone apartment in 1970. Looking taller than his height of five feet ten inches, he was slim, physically firm, with graying hair. His face within a fraction of a second could exhibit a succession of delight, awareness, and curiosity. He listened attentively. I found him utterly charming. A dazzlingly intelligent psychiatrist . . . and no surprise that he would be an intimate of the brilliant Huxley.

To establish the EWI I created the Mens Sana Publishing Co. In my off-hours, evenings, and weekends, I edited the manuscript for the manual needed by psychiatrists to administer the test, laid out the pages, and had it printed.

In the EWI questionnaire, patients were asked if certain phrases described their own inner feelings.

I am so weary of myself that life seems a burden.

I cannot forget the mess I have made of my life.

The world would be a better place without me.

The test itself turned out to have an unexpected therapeutic value. The schizophrenia sufferer was reading or hearing words used by other schizophrenics to describe their acute distress. For a person living in a lonely, bizarre, terrifying mind-world it's immensely comforting to learn that he or she is not alone. *Out there are other sufferers like me, people who have visions and thoughts similar to mine.*

Knowing that "I am not alone" can bring huge relief to the deeply depressed mind, says Dr. Cynthia Bisbee, one of the editors of Psychedelic Prophets. An early user of the EWI, Dr. Bisbee worked alongside Osmond when he moved to Alabama.

Indicative of suicidal impulse among people diagnosed with schizophrenia are statements like:

I expect very little from life.

I am a failure.

I would have been better off if I were somebody else.

By scoring patients' responses to such statements and four hundred others, it was possible for El-Meligi and Osmond reliably to predict if a person were at risk of committing suicide. If successfully marketed, the EWI arguably would speed mental-health professionals toward earlier detection of a patient's potential for suicide, toward earlier intervention, and therefore saving lives.

More than three million Americans suffer disabling schizophrenia. One in twenty of them—roughly 175,000 sufferers of paranoia and other severe forms of schizophrenia—are prone to suicide. Could the number have been reduced if the EWI had been actively and extensively used? Going back to 1970, by how much?

"It's not a stretch," Dr. Bisbee told me, "to say that many lives lost to suicide could have been saved, had the EWI become a standardized test."

Regrettably the test failed to gain traction in the psychiatric community. Perhaps because of Osmond's reputation in the controversial world of psychedelics, standard medical test publishers wouldn't undertake to produce and market the EWI. Or maybe I was to blame. While I was equipped to edit the EWI manual, I should not have allowed myself to be recruited into manufacturing and selling the testing materials. It was work for which I was singularly unqualified, to say nothing of the fact that I had a full-time job editing two national sports magazines at the time.

Moneim El-Meligi, for one, was angry at my failure. Gracious, outgoing, curious, El-Meligi had given me help in diagnosing my troubled son, who was at risk of suicide. As a teenager, he began to suffer from severe, escalating depression. A week before I met El-Meligi for the first time, my son had lain on a Vermont country road in the hope a truck would run over him. His excessive use of drugs, including LSD, was to blame, I thought. But a genetic disorder may have played a role.

"It's really unpardonable," El-Meligi told me. "Members of your family have known for years of inherited mental illness that has passed down from generation to generation. And evidently no one spoke of it. Your son is likely the latest victim."

My curiosity aroused, I researched and wrote a biography of my great-grandfather, Henry Fry, *A Mind at Sea*, published by Canada's Dundurn Press in 2012. When he was twenty-three years old, Henry recorded the fact that he'd suffered a nervous breakdown, resulting in severe depression. His illness, he confessed, mirrored that of his own father, and in 1877 he suffered a melancholy so intense that he was admitted to the Hartford Retreat for the Insane in Connecticut. There he was kept under careful watch for potential suicide.

Thinks he cannot live long, recorded the hospital's admission record. *Very despondent . . . Attendant told not to leave him unattended. Leave his door open . . .*

Henry Fry eventually escaped his madness and went on to write essays on politics and economics, and a book about the earliest steam navigation of the North Atlantic. He died in 1897. His widow, my great-grandmother, lived another thirty-six years, witnessing the suicides of two of her six sons. Then came my own birth, who fortunately was not born with the flawed gene, surviving to write this book with its chapter on suicide.

As I see so many friends suffer and die in their latter years, I wonder how eventually it will be for me. I have a living will, signed and notarized, that defines what doctors and hospitals cannot do to keep me alive when death is certain. I'm uncertain, though, that it will enable me to avoid the degrading, prolonged illnesses of the very aged. It's a desire increasingly sought by Americans, who are still alive from the baby-boom generation born during the twenty years following World War II. According to a Gallup Poll, three out of four of them say a doctor should be allowed to end a terminally ill patient's life by painless means if the patient requests it. But because euthanasia is broadly outlawed, the patient doesn't get relief. Some may deliberately end their lives by overdosing medications, even poisoning themselves.

The ethos of the sanctity of life, embedded in our laws and medicine, is waning. Hopefully freed from the influence of a theocracy opposed to euthanasia, politicians will enact laws to allow doctors to collaborate in enabling women and men, who are certain to die, to terminate their lives. A transformation is surely coming, as it did with the gender revolution.

"An impossible idea becomes possible, then becomes necessary, and then all but a handful of diehards accept its inevitability" are words employed in connection with gay marriage by the Canadian writer and my fellow McGill University alum Adam Gopnik.

"The tipping point is that magic moment when an idea, trend or social behavior crosses a threshold, tips and spreads like wildfire," writes Malcolm Gladwell, another immigrant from Canada like myself.

Allowed to lessen the physical torment of death, doctors will be free to improve the quality of life by easing our passage from it.

CHAPTER 11

MURDER, REMORSE, REDEMPTION

What I learned from a man who killed his wife.
The Warders with their shoes of felt
Crept by each padlocked door,
And peeped and saw, with eyes of awe,
Grey figures on the floor,
And wondered why men knelt to pray
Who never prayed before.

"The Ballad of Reading Gaol," Oscar Wilde

Between the years 2015 to 2018 I exchanged letters with one of the most perceptive, widely read persons I know, a man who once replicated the crime O.J. Simpson was tried for. Married to an attractive wife, inflamed by jealousy, he killed her. Unlike Simpson,

Leonard is white and he confessed to the murder. The judge gave him twenty-two years to life.

Until I met Leonard, "shame" and "remorse" were merely words in my vocabulary. Like most of us, I would guess, I've not experienced a personal tragedy comparable to Leonard's. Weird as it is to say, he demonstrated how unfortunate I may be in not having been truly unfortunate. Described by him, shame and remorse and self-reflecting disgust took on a meaning with searing aliveness. He showed how they can penetrate to the core of a person's life, leading to a transformative upheaval in it.

"I came to prison," Leonard wrote, "with an opinionated head, a closed-down heart, and a defensive body. I became broad-minded and teachable."

I have exchanged dozens of letters with him, and visited him twice in prison. A lean six feet, he is physically fit, clean-shaven, friendly, well-mannered, at ease in conversation. While we were together in the visitors room at the prison, I felt we might easily have been outside in a Starbucks drinking coffee.

Leonard is not his real name. Revealing it might negatively influence conditions of his release. At nearly sixty years of age, after thirty years of incarceration, he was eventually granted parole.

A graduate of the New York Theological Seminary, a degree that he obtained while imprisoned, Leonard thinks that, unlike himself, I am a lost soul—someone to be pitied for my void of faith and for my incessant criticism of organized religion. Being censured by a prison inmate for my religious shortcomings was laden with irony . . . the non-criminal seen at a lower level than the criminal. But in Leonard I came face to face with the enigmatic way in which the incarcerated and the free, the imprisoned and un-imprisoned, can occupy the same spiritual space.

About twenty percent of New York state's 46,000 prisoners are "lifers" like Leonard, serving terms from twenty years to life. The prisons are mostly located in the otherwise attractive landscape of upstate New York. Pastureland, sinuous riverbanks, hills and mountains are acned in places with the forbidding, turreted, razorblade-wire-topped, dark concrete walls of fifty or more correctional facilities, once called penitentiaries. The penitentiary name has been abandoned, presumably because most prisoners are thought to be incapable of being penitent or of feeling remorse. Rather their behavior can be corrected now by such clever methods as nitpicking rules, solitary confinement, and mass punishment imposed as a result of a single prisoner's violation.

My home is near Sing Sing and even closer to the famous Bedford Women's Prison, which once housed the diet doctor murderess Jean Harris, and Amy Fisher who shot Joey Buttafuoco's wife. Around town, I know local actors, musicians, artists, stage producers, and clerics who've volunteered their time counseling prisoners, instructing them in a program called Rehabilitation Through the Arts (RTA). Many have been in prison since they were teenagers, void of normal adult development. RTA addresses their lack of social skills. Through stage productions and other programs, they learn teamwork, conflict resolution, and real-world communication. Inmates who participate in RTA, upon release from prison, are ten times less likely than nonparticipants to violate parole or to repeat a crime. Their recidivism rate is seven percent, compared to more than fifty percent for most state prisoners across the U.S.

In my eighty-fifth year I suggested to a Presbyterian pastor friend Hans Hallundbaek, whose wife Katherine Vockins started RTA, that I might employ my editing and writing skills to assist prisoners in telling their stories.

"I have this idea," I told Hans, "of working with prisoners who are studying religion, mainly theological school graduates. A leap of faith is more likely to have happened with this kind of inmate. I want to help them write their stories."

The book would surely be a bestseller, I dreamed. Prisoners who transformed themselves through Christ. And so I began to write to inmates.

At first, things looked promising. I heard from a guy with a Mafia-sounding name who'd served forty years of a murder sentence. Another was a prisoner who was going to be deported to Jamaica upon his release. Another was fighting a wrongful conviction.

Another was out of prison and attending Yale Divinity School. None of them, I eventually discovered, was willing to put in the time-consuming, difficult work of writing to me about their imprisonment and pursuit of religion.

One guy, out on parole and doing community work, was especially discouraging. "I would say," he wrote to me, "that religious conversion proclaimed by prisoners is often viewed as inauthentic and suspicious by parole boards, prison staff, and other prisoners. I have seen many times someone who was very religious while incarcerated having nothing to do with religion when he got out." Here was troubling news, suggesting that my bestselling book scheme was foolish if not infeasible.

Two prisoners, however, did take me up on my invitation. One was a lifer, James Morse, whose story I tell in the chapter that follows this one. The other was Leonard. Over his many years in prison, he had been a mentor and positive role model for younger inmates.

He appeared to have enjoyed a childhood suffused in religion. His father was a pastor of an evangelical congregation. As a teenager he was a star athlete in high school. Over the years, I noticed, he'd lost little of his lean muscularity and athleticism. His teenage mind, however, had been infected with a toxic, aggressive virus. It started when he was playing basketball. He punched guys who were roughing him as he went for a layup. The desire to retaliate by punching an opponent escalated. During the six months leading up to his crime his feelings rose to an obsessive desire to kill.

"I planned to kill several other people . . . I can't remember who," he confessed to me.

At the age of twenty-five he had married a young woman whom he'd loved almost since his early teens. She told him that she'd always wanted to marry him. But before their marriage, she'd had a long relationship with another guy. Someone religious, she told Leonard.

A virgin at the time of their marriage, Leonard discovered that his wife's description of her former boyfriend as a religious person was untrue. His suspicions were aroused. Maybe she'd had sexual relations with the guy. A couple of years into their marriage, Leonard came to the conviction that she was having an affair. The knowledge of it, though false, made him impotent. There arose in him again the seething need to avenge.

He waited for a day when she didn't exercise at her health club, but rather came home directly from work. When she did, he strangled her with a belt. He propped up her corpse on the front passenger seat of his car, and drove fifty miles away from their home, depositing her lifeless body at the back of a store. Then he phoned the police to inform them that his wife was missing.

Three days later, overcome with contrition, Leonard drove to the police station and voluntarily confessed. After fingerprinting, he was handcuffed and shoved into a cell with other criminals.

"I watched as the steel door was slammed shut in my face," he wrote to me. "The next morning I awoke from sleeping on a urine-stained mattress in a filthy holding cell filled with men awaiting court appearance.

"I'd just committed a murder so terrible that I couldn't bear the shame of what I'd done. For almost two weeks in county jail I lay under my covers in bed in the fetal position, crying uncontrollably. I never knew a person could cry so many hours in a row and not run out of tears. I wanted nothing except to end my existence, to crush my skull against the concrete wall of this dirty, musty-smelling county jail cell.

"How to do it within sight of an officer who was on a suicide watch of me? I decided to pretend I was going to the toilet. I would put my back to the wall, bend at the waist, and run as hard as I could across the cell into the opposite wall, breaking my neck.

"Then it happened. 'There's another way.' I heard the voice of the Holy Spirit. 'There's another way for you. Turn your life over to me.' I was lying on the stinking mattress staring up at the bottom of the bunk bed overhead, still thinking of the futility of living. Then I heard the Holy Spirit say it again. 'There's another way. Turn your life back over to me.'

"At first, I didn't know how to respond. My heart throbbed. I paused. I finally answered, almost out loud, 'I will, Lord, no matter what.' Immediately I felt a tremendous burden lift from me.

"It was the beginning of a life behind bars that has transfigured me."

Possessed of a keen intelligence and curiosity, Leonard worked for many years in the prison library. He earned a bachelor of arts degree *summa cum laude* from Bard College. His reading of philosophy and religious works was voluminous. He wrote, preached, and taught Church history. He immersed himself in the writings of Dietrich Bonhoeffer and Reinhold Niebuhr.

"If I'd remained outside jail walls, I would have settled comfortably into the institutional religiousness of my childhood upbringing, without ever entering into deep, authentic spirituality. Imprisonment, while outwardly punishing, has transformed me inwardly. I am no longer the person once convicted of homicide."

"What people learn from your experience?" I asked him.

"It's how to come to terms with the sins you've committed. Dealing with shame and remorse is to grow, to realize that you have become a person who could never do such things again, come to terms with the life you once lived, live your life differently, not be capable of the sins and errors of your past. You need to describe your character honestly. Would you want people to see it described on a giant screen?"

His prison existence was defined in another way. Leonard was a white man living in a largely black world. More than half of his fellow prisoners were African Americans. He composed a book advising young men, in and out of prison, on how to avoid attacks—face cutting—by assailants using broken bottles or jagged pieces of metal to rip faces. He wrote a two-volume history about racism's invention and how to combat it. In prison, he escaped the bigotry that might have infected him if he'd been living, as he once did, in an economically depressed area of white working people.

"I learned the importance of the Golden Rule," he wrote, "to love others, to be tolerant . . . even in Sing Sing where the violence among prisoners is terrifying."

Twenty years into his sentence Leonard's correspondence with a relative in Israel turned his mind to the Jewishness of Jesus. He became a Messianic Jew, believing that Christ, yes, was the long-awaited Messiah, just not born of a virgin or part of the Trinity. He came to observe strict Hebraic customs and holy days. Odd, I reflected, that a prison inmate, severely constricted in his movements, would choose to enter a religion in order to have his life severely restricted by a strict, intricate web of rules.

"I'm not about to contest your beliefs," I wrote him. "Hopefully the Jesus of the Messianic Jews is the same Jesus as the one who forgave you when you were lying in your jail cell after the murder." The thought clearly gave him no satisfaction.

"I think it would be wise," he wrote to me, "to no longer discuss the Bible, religion, etc. You are miles away from where I stand on religion—too much of a gap to come to any mutual understanding.

"Look, I can never bring back to life the person whose life I ended. I have done, and am doing, all in my power since that terrible day to redress my shame and sin."

In retrospect, Leonard likely had been suffering obsessive-compulsive disorder. OCD had propelled him on a homicidal pathway that he could not resist. He failed to seek an attorney who might have entered an insanity plea.

After twenty-five years he was eligible for parole. Five times before skeptical, politically appointed parole board members, under intense pressure not to release a murderer back into public life, Leonard was compelled to recite the horrific details of his crime. To these strangers he must convey a credible sense of shame and disgust about killing his wife. Most lifers fail at it because of an inability to express their thoughts clearly, lack of insight into what they did, inability to envision something they have done as it is seen by another person. A simple lack of education is typically at fault. Statistically, incarcerated for the same crime, an educated prisoner is more likely to gain a favorable verdict from a parole board. Unsurprisingly, Leonard performed well. He failed to gain his release, however. His wife's family never forgave him. They were present at every parole board hearing that took place after his twenty-fifth year in prison, announcing the pain they still felt from the loss of their daughter.

Finally they relented, expressing no opposition to Leonard's release. A parole board, reformed under New York State Governor Mario Cuomo, granted Leonard his freedom. His extraordinary work benefiting other prisoners was a reason for his release. Another is New York state's concern about an increasingly aging prison population. Taxpayers are burdened with the soaring medical costs of caring for elderly inmates. The organization RAPP (Release Aging People in Prison) is leading a campaign to get parole and freedom for prisoners like Leonard. Recidivism is negligible among older criminals, including those convicted of homicide, who have served long terms. The horror of their long imprisonment dominates their minds, virtually ensuring that once out on the street they will do nothing that might put them back behind bars.

"I now hate violence in any form," Leonard told me when we shared a coffee at Starbucks in a town where he's not living. "I have such disgust over the violence I committed that I can't even look at a football game."

The employees where he has worked have proven, in their wariness and hostility, to be not that different from most of the guards he encountered in prison.

Leonard's dream is to go to divinity school and become a prison chaplain. He relates to me his adaptation of a famous story told by a rabbi. In Leonard's version, the rabbi is approached by a young man obsessed with guilt over his sins.

"What should I do?" he asked.

The rabbi answered. "Go home, find a soft pillow, take it with you on a walk, pull out the feathers, and cast them around, even let them scatter in the breeze. When you have done that, come back and see me."

The young man returned.

"I have done as you told me. What do I now do?"

"Go back out and pick up the feathers."

"But that's impossible," cried the young man.

"It's the effort you must make with all the sins and mistakes you made in life."

CHAPTER 12

THE TIME OF OUR LIVES

When you forget what time it is, where you are, and forget your own body—
spiritually you are everywhere.

Anonymous author, *Cloud of Unknowing*, late fourteenth century

The separation between past, present, and future is only an illusion,
although a convincing one.

Albert Einstein

A few months after meeting Leonard, encountered in the previous chapter, I received a letter from James E. Morse (his real name). An African American prisoner, Morse was writing to me from the sick ward of the Fishkill Correctional Facility in Beacon, on the east bank of the Hudson River, fifty miles upstream from Manhattan. His home for forty years had been a barred room the size of a large closet, usually shared with another prisoner.

Morse enclosed a picture of himself, a wiry, thin man with bony, dark skin and curious eyes shining from behind heavily framed glasses. In twilight you'd see a Spike Lee doppelganger.

Morse wrote to me that he was undergoing kidney dialysis twice weekly while suffering heart disease as well. He'd netted only one dollar from his last robbery. It was his fifth conviction, however, requiring the judge to sentence him to life imprisonment.

Morse was born and raised in abject poverty and neglect in East Harlem amid gang violence. His circumstances were so dire—a drug-addicted mother, abandoning stepfathers, one move after another to foster homes, arriving in prison at age seventeen—that he preferred not to describe it to me. "Use your imagination and double the horror," he told me.

I found Morse a remarkably good writer. From reading his letters, you'd think that he'd attended a soigné New England prep school, grooming students in etiquette. "This day, I received your letter," he wrote. "Thank you immensely. Attached is a copy of my journal entry, using a nom de plume."

Over time, I keenly awaited his letters. On a sunlit spring day in 2017, I was in my windowless home office editing Morse's semiauto-biographical account of his first entering prison. I'd been doing so now for several months, off and on, reorienting his poignant words to read more fluidly. I'd just marked a paragraph whose meaning was uncertain, and was writing a note to Morse that he must explain it, when I heard the letter carrier's steps outside. As usual, I climbed the stairs from my office, went to the mailbox, and opened it. I immediately spotted a brown envelope that I'd mailed to Morse two weeks earlier, containing an edited essay he'd written.

Scrawled on the envelope was the word *DECEASED*.

During the time it had taken the U.S. Post Office to deliver my package to Morse, he had died. By now, I realized, he was likely already interred in a potter's field next to a prison, the inscription on the stone his prisoner ID, 99A2830.

I opened the return envelope from the prison office, and read again the words of praise I'd written to Morse about a short story he'd sent me. Entitled "The Square Fetter," the story is about a man named Jones after he was sentenced by a judge and was entering prison. Morse wrote:

> *Months after Jones' strange day in court, he still cringed at the sound of the tap, tap rapping of the woman judge's time-sick gavel; the tap, tap that foretold Jones' sentence to the living death; the crazed tapping that accompanied his transport to the non-penitential, non-reforming institution called the "Beast" by the captives who languish in that ruinous fetter.*

I'd asked Morse if he himself was Jones. "Every prisoner is Jones," he responded, "one who is forced into surrender, even sickeningly embracing it." On the wall of Morse's cell a previous inmate had inscribed the words, "I like this shit." That an incarcerated person could come to "like this shit," wrote Morse, was actually surrender . . .

> . . . the first step in the merging of Jones' soul with the vile binding force of the square fetter. In it he would become a wretched object of insignificance, one more institutional thingamajig.

At the conclusion of his story, Morse added a commentary about a phenomenon known as chronophobia.

> Fear of time may be the most common anxiety disorder of prison inmates. Terrified by the enclosure and restraint, what appears to be claustrophobia is really chronophobia. The prisoner becomes terrified by the duration and immensity of time. The combined effect of imprisonment's duration and its pinched space tampers with the inmost being of the human.

What impressed me was the realization that Morse himself, though understanding he would die in prison, had found the key to his own escape. They could incarcerate his body, but not his mind. A man who spent most of his life locked in prison concluded that he could find freedom by escaping the bond of time.

"Suppose everyone's a prisoner?" asked Morse. "What if everyone suffers fear of time?" The statement caught my eye. The idea is expressed in *A Secular Age* by the Canadian philosopher Charles Taylor, who was briefly my fraternity brother at McGill University.

"We have constructed an environment," writes Taylor, "in which we live uniform univocal time, which we try to measure and control in order to get things done. This 'time frame' deserves . . . Max Weber's famous description, 'iron cage.'" Millions live their lives frenetically tied to time, trying to perform useful tasks in less time.

Weber's iron cage was a form of Morse's square fetter. Someone outside of a prison can lead a life as imprisoned as someone within. Prisoner and captor can be alike in sanity or insanity, an irony central to the 1999 movie *The Green Mile*, based on a Stephen King novel.

My own precious time is running out. More and more of it is absorbed in merely sustaining a successfully functioning body Remembering the timing of pills taken during the day. Physiotherapy. Coping with the labyrinthine health-care bureaucracy. Waiting in doctors' offices.

Acute is the anxious awareness of tasks that must be accomplished before I suffer an incapacitating illness, dementia, stroke, die. Will I get it all done before the train leaves the station? There are still articles to write, advice to give to my children and grandchildren, arguments to settle, forgivenesses to render. Time is running out.

CHAPTER 13

KILLED BY BELIEF

"All three monotheisms praise Abraham for being willing to hear voices and then to take his son on a long and rather mad and gloomy walk. And then the caprice by which his murderous hand is finally stayed is written down as divine mercy. I find a father holding a knife to his son's throat to show his love to a totalitarian dictator wicked!"

Christopher Hitchens

I suffer *somnum interruptus*, sleeping one, two, or three hours at a stretch, then waking up. The cause of my interrupted sleep is not a stomach ache or back pain. An idea has erupted in my brain. A singular fresh thought is buzzing in my mind like a petulant child crying for attention. I get up, write it down on a pad of paper, then return to bed.

At six a.m. on my eighty-seventh birthday I rolled out of bed, my head bursting with an idea that would sizzle on Netflix. The plot would involve a human calamity, linked to the famous Old Testament story of Abraham's willingness to slaughter his own son in order to satisfy a demand from God.

To kill another human is the epitome of sin, one of the prohibitions of the Ten Commandments, punishable by death in the electric chair. Yet the Book of Genesis encourages the idea that homicide is permissible if God says it's okay. Faith trumps morality.

For the Netflix movie I had a clear, keen notion of what the visual and the acting would be like. Murray Abraham would be perfect to act as the progenitor of Judaism, Christianity, and Islam. Instead of playing Mozart-envying Salieri, a solemn, wrinkled, ashen-faced Abraham (Murray) would portray his homonym, seed of the three monotheistic religions, leading his son Isaac, played by Dustin Hoffman, up a rocky hillside outside of Jerusalem. Hoffman—sorry, wrong, Isaac—would be terror-stricken, and frankly pissed off. Abraham had tricked him . . . never told him several days ago about what he intended to do. If he had—Isaac was no dummy—he wouldn't have agreed to travel for three days with his father, on donkeys, in the heat, to this godforsaken mountain, and then allow his hands and feet to be bound with rope. What had he done to the old man to make him act like this? Where was the lamb that Abraham was going to barbecue on that pyre of dry sticks over there?

"No lamb, son," said Abraham, who was now brandishing a knife over Isaac's face. "You. God has told me to sacrifice you."

The idea of the movie excited me. I could hardly wait to finish breakfast and go downstairs to my computer to start work on the script. Maybe I'd pitch it to movie director Norman Jewison, who once directed me in a skit performed in the Banff Spring Hotel employees summer show. I already anticipated what I'd sell to Norm…an updated twenty-first century version of the Abraham-Isaac story.

In the Biblical segment of the film, Murray Abraham, his wrinkled face radiating agony and ecstasy, waits long enough to hear God withdraw his command to sacrifice Isaac. "Lay off the kid. I was only testing the depth of your faith," says God. "I wanted to see if you'd go so far as to kill your own child if I told you to."

In the modern segment of the film, I will go on to replicate Abraham's story in the sky, far above the Biblical mountain. The action takes place in a Boeing Dreamliner with two hundred passengers who are 35,000 feet in the air, jetting to Riyadh. The camera zooms in on a man with a wan, bearded face, eyes brimming with hostility. Then comes the voiceover—solemn, deep-throated, authoritative. Allah is heard instructing Ibn, or whatever is his name, "Go to the front of the plane. Take out your knife. Kill the men in the pilot's cabin, as I instruct you."

Will the assassin succeed in causing the airliner to crash, resulting in the deaths of all the passengers including his own son whom he'd brought on board with him? Allahu Akbar!

Or will there be a last-minute reversal? Will Ibn change his mind? What should be the film's denouement?

In my excitement and uncertainty, even though it was only eight-thirty in the morning, I called my friend, Louis Dupre, retired T. Lawrason Riggs Professor of Religion at Yale University, and the author of no fewer than twenty-one books on philosophy and religion. I excitedly told him about my movie idea, even though I feared that he might view it as a foolish scheme.

"What's the difference, Louis," I asked, "between Abraham hearing God's voice instructing him to kill his son, and a zealot in an airplane hearing God's voice instructing him to assassinate the pilot?"

"None," quietly replied Louis.

"Yes, but as you know, Abraham's readiness to sacrifice his child is a stunning example not only of an orthodox Old Testament teaching but of Soren Kierkegaard's thought: the truly religious person's leap of faith takes him out of the ethical realm."

"What does it say about a religion, Louis, when one must look somewhere outside it to evaluate whether an action performed in its name is good or evil?"

"Calm yourself, John. It's just a story."

"Yes, but a helluva movie, don't you think?"

"Why, dear boy? Everyone knows the ending."

CHAPTER 14

END TALK

All men should strive to learn before they die,

what they are running from, and to, and why.

James Thurber

I said I was hoping to die in my sleep, but Saul responded by saying that, on the

contrary, he would like to die wide awake and fully conscious, because death is

such a crucial experience he wouldn't want to miss it.

A conversation with Saul Bellow reported by Amos Oz

I attend Death Cafés where people, typically strangers, gather to eat cake, drink tea and coffee, and discuss for a couple of hours the issues surrounding death. Additionally, I belong to a small, intimate group of older men and women who discuss the challenges of aging. This chapter is a window into these encounters . . . a raw amalgam of the words spoken and my own occasionally raffish observations.

At a Death Café, six or seven men and women typically sit around a table conversing about assisted living, hospice care, where to get suicide pills. We discuss religious funerals versus nonreligious memorials, leaving money to ungrateful children, the cost of gravestones, bankruptcy for affordable nursing care, who's a good lawyer to do my will.

Although the Death Café name may suggest otherwise, the talk isn't all gloom and doom. Much of it turns toward addressing the challenge of living one's life better and more meaningfully. Born in 2004 as Café Mortel, it was the idea of French Swiss anthropologist Bernard Cretazz. He thought of it as a casual forum where people, often strangers, could bat around philosophical thoughts. By increasing their awareness of death they would "make more of their finite lives."

At a recent Death Café in our village, across from me sat three attractive women in their seventies—"recovering Roman Catholics," one laughed. Next to her, a wiry little guy with a sunny smile said that he was a hypnotherapist . . . fishing for clients, no doubt. Seated next to me, a tall man with an angry face introduced himself as someone who'd seen lots of death in Vietnam. He'd witnessed men, women, and children shot or burned to death.

At the end of the table a Jewish spinster in her 60s, grey hair, stubby, with a cheerful mien and loud voice, confessed that she'd grown up in a home full of hate, not love. "I've done everything in my life to overcome my past," she said, "yoga, theater acting, meditation, breathing."

One of the women declared that she had joined the Presbyterian Church. "I need a community to belong to," she said, as she shook a wayward lock of her carefully coiffed jet-black hair away from her left eye. "What do you all want to know about me anyway? I grew up in Puerto Rico. We openly acknowledged death, even celebrate it."

"You're lucky," interjected woman number two in a weepy voice, her narrow, angular face framing eyes alternately expressing happiness and anxiety. "We never discussed death in our family. When I once wanted to talk about it, my aunt admonished me. 'Darling, we don't discuss that sort of thing.'"

A grimace of disapproval clouded the face of a young woman, plump, wearing glasses, with prematurely graying hair. "I think all the time about death," she said. "I've seen so much tragedy and bad outcomes. In college my roommate committed suicide. I'm not sure if there's a life after death. I wonder about the rest of my life. Will it get worse? Life isn't fair."

What words might relieve the unhappiness of this morose, healthy, well-fed woman with no evident economic problems, complaining about life's unfairness?

"Sure, life is unreasonable and unfair," I said. Heads around the table swiveled toward me. "It takes courage to go on living. I mean, you're one tiny person, living on a speck of a planet that's a speck in the universe, with no idea of what it all means. Okay, God has disappointed you. But most likely he's the God that Job faced, basically indifferent to your suffering. So buck up."

Tears welled in the young woman's eyes. Clearly my impromptu, remarkably insensitive little speech had only served to deepen her anxiety and unhappiness. As I ruminated on what I'd said that was wrong, the guy who'd been a medic in Vietnam, maybe in his seventies now, his facial skin lined like a scratched piece of slate, began a soliloquy on deaths in his family.

Huge, he said, was his wife's funeral just eight months ago, held in an austere Methodist church. The service had been elaborate, hundreds in attendance. He took ten minutes to tell us about it. Then he told of his mother's funeral, another extended monologue. Then an uncle . . . that was an elaborate going-away for the corpus. The boredom at the table was palpable. "You poor man," the ladies sighed in unified sympathy. "You must be grieving terribly."

"I told myself to shape up," responded the widower, he who had witnessed so much death in Vietnam. "I get through it by being tough. I don't allow myself to be weepy or sorrowful."

Across the table, the Jewish lady confessed that she was embarrassed. "I want to be cremated. I read in today's *New York Times* that half of all people are now choosing to have their bodies cremated.

Traditional Judaism says it's wrong. I don't know what to tell my son. I haven't even got a will. I can't seem to get started on one. I can't find a lawyer I trust."

This statement immediately drew a response from a thickset middle-aged woman, shoulders sloping to a box-like torso in a pink sweater, a pancake-flat face, silvery white hair, who'd just seated herself at the table.

"I'm a licensed attorney in New York and Florida," she said in a commanding voice. "You can talk to me about it. Or I can give you the names of a couple of other attorneys." The woman spoke with assurance, her words made credible by piercing eyes and a voice radiating authority.

"You need to list and photograph everything in your house, and specify what goes to whom. I've seen the most terrible arguments, families turn to hatred, dishonoring their dead parents because they didn't specify how stuff is to be inherited."

"Wow!" exclaimed one of the women. "I was just going to leave it to my kids to sort for themselves who gets what. Was I wrong!"

"Has everyone written an outline of how they want their funeral or memorial to be handled?" asked the attorney. Before anyone could respond, however, a bell rang signaling the day's Death Café had ended. Leaning forward across the table, the attorney asked me if I knew of an inexpensive room to rent in our village. The sanest, most pragmatic, most helpful person at the table needed a place to live.

And what of these others at the table, strangers, who had shared with me their intimate thoughts and feelings about death? What lives truly lay behind their words?

The week following the Death Café, I attended a noontime, bring-your-own luncheon of our aging group. We're three men and four women, average age slightly less than octogenarian, who meet monthly in one of our homes to talk about the issues facing us in old age.

"What's on your mind?" asked our discussion leader, at the age of eighty never lacking in ideas of how-to-live-your-life-better, his gentle eyes brimming intelligence and curiosity. "Today let's describe our personal progress from childhood to adulthood. In no more than eight minutes each. I'll start with myself."

He'd lived his early adult years as a Romantic, or as a twentieth-century suburban version of a Romantic, he explained in a soft monotone. Then came the crisis. His wife left him. Following the divorce, he moved to a Buddhist compound in the Catskills, better known to the world as a training ground for Jewish comedians. Here he learned to form real, not transactional, friendships, he said. The group sighed in solemn approval.

My wife, a German immigrant, breathlessly delivered her eight-minute autobiography. She'd been a child in the World War II Hitler years, sent to the mountains to escape Munich's bombing, visible as flashes in the night sky. She remembered mostly the strong women in her family, aunts who ran clothing stores while their husbands were on the front being shot at, or themselves shooting at a variety of Himmler-designated dispensable ethnic populations. Three weeks after embarking from the *S.S. United States* in New York harbor, she met the man whom she'd allow herself to marry, a divorced father of two children, an editor.

And there I was. The women in the group eagerly anticipated hearing the story as told by the son-of-a-bitch who'd robbed the previous speaker of her family's genetic disposition to strong female independence. They were not to be gratified. The clever fellow steered his speech away from the awkward subject. Rather I talked solemnly about how the Danish existentialist Soren Kierkegaard and Ernest Becker's *Denial of Death* have influenced my thinking.

"Oh yes, these late years have been the best of my life," I sighed. Probably not the best years for Mrs. German immigrant, the women suspected, squirming in their chairs. One woman realized it was her turn to tell the group of her life.

"I'm a recovering Roman Catholic," she smiled. Murmurs of appreciation. Of course, it was agreed, recovery is monstrously diffi-cult for someone attempting to leave an organization of frocked men who've buggered young boys.

Gaunt-faced, she spoke angrily of her years, joyous until she lost her husband a dozen years ago. He must have been a *helluva* guy because after he was gone she collapsed in total lonely despond. She saw a wonderful psychiatrist who cured her. Well, not really, she confessed. Living alone can be miserable.

"Why does this just happen to women?" I asked.

"Because they live longer lives," chorused the ladies, suppressing the collective urge to cry out "you stupid."

"Wrong!" I exclaimed. "A life-expectancy statistic is unrelated to a person's ability to live a happy or a miserable existence. Any idiot would know that."

"I just turned seventy-three," said one of the women ruefully. She had a determined look, green eyes, shocking white hair, lean and fit for her age. "I'm still working, though fewer hours. What's it going to be like when I stop going to the office entirely, retire?"

We sat silently waiting for her to answer her own question. After all, she was a professional social worker, counseling people on how to solve and cope with problems in their everyday lives. Her answer would be illuminating, I thought. But she answered with another question. "What purpose will I find in my life?" No one spoke. We were stunned. A woman, who helped other people answer troubling questions, couldn't answer her own.

Our host for the day was a retired school psychologist. Jim had spent most of his professional life counseling young people. He wanted to speak about his own life, he said.

"When I was a young man, I was adventurous, intentionally naïve so that my mind would absorb all kinds of thoughts and experiences. I shipped out on freighters across the Pacific. I lived in Japan and Africa."

Late in life, he confessed, he'd become a skeptic. "Facts, verifiable facts are all that count. Beliefs result in nothing but backward, barbaric, destructive behavior.

"Now I have something to tell you," he concluded. His voice had become strained, squeaky, hinting at an illness affecting his ability to speak.

"I'm going to die sometime within the next six months to a year." "Whaaat!" we cried. "It can't be."

"I have ALS. You know, the paralyzing Lou Gehrig's disease." He looked around the table. Mute, we stared at him.

"I lived for 85 years. Even without ALS, how much more was I really going to get out of life? Only increasing frailty. I can no longer indulge my love of travel. I've gotten through the cornerstones of love and work, of which Freud said, 'That's all there is.' I've had a good marriage, a loving and successful family, thriving grandchildren, and an interesting helpful profession.

"That's all there is."

CHAPTER 15

COMMUNING AND CONSOLING

The nearest friends can go

With anyone to death, comes so far short

They might as well not try to go at all.

No, from the time when one is sick to death,

One is alone, and he dies more alone.

Friends make pretense of following to the grave,

But before one is in it, their minds are turned

And making the best of their way back to life

And living people, and things they understand.

Robert Frost, "Home Burial"

When my father lay dying in 1983 from complications of emphysema, I sat beside him in the hospital's intensive-care unit. He was hooked to a breathing device, his arms stuck with plastic tubes intravenously feeding him nutrients and god-knows-what medications. The nurses had placed a blackboard by his bed so that Dad could respond to questions, communicate his wishes. On it he had scrawled, "End this. Stop it!" No one had.

My mother had beseeched me to fly to Montreal to persuade the doctors to do as my father wished . . . to be detached from the cruel form of life support, sophisticated in its engineering, utterly crude and insensitive to the human being kept alive. We'd become entrapped in what has become a common, painful situation. The sophisticated medical technology that keeps sufferers alive creates conflicts. Between patients' families and doctors. Among spouses and children. Among lawyers and hospitals. And among doctors themselves.

At the hospital, I spoke to three doctors. They refused to take responsibility for the euthanasia of yanking the life support from him. The situation was awkward in another way. I had meager emotional attachment to my father. I had been a disobedient child, fought against his wishes. It was he who telegraphed to me in Gosport, England, on the eve of sailing into the stormy English Channel, with a desperate plea for me to abandon my foolish scheme (Chapter 3). Even when I achieved professional success as an editor, he remarked to a friend of mine, "Look at John. What have we done wrong?" Display of love was meager. We were at a distance. Now this man needed my help so that he could end his life.

I was in the ICU on a night when I spotted the physician in

116

charge, an Egyptian with a kindly face, attentive and listening as I spoke to him. I pointed at the blackboard. "Please, on behalf of me and our family, do what my father clearly wants. He wants to die." After questioning me further, he agreed.

"Make him suffer as little as possible," I pleaded.

"Yes, we'll give him morphine." The doctor gently removed the breathing apparatus from my father's face. The tubes were detached.

Now I moved my head close to my father's face. "Dad, it's okay now. They will let you go." I continued, disguising any wavering indecision that might have been evident in my voice. "Thank you for all you have done for me. You have been a good father."

In consoling and commiserating with friends as they were dying, I've rarely had much more success than what I experienced with my father. Over a period of a year, I spent hours on the phone with a ninety-year-old friend, attempting to talk him out of his desire to end his life. Timothy Tung was a Chinese-born librarian and journalist who in 1980 had accompanied me on a trip to the northeastern mountains of the former Manchuria. Now Tim's body was racked with the pain of acute shingles. His frail wife had died next to him in bed after they'd argued.

Tim now only wanted to die himself. He swallowed a dozen Ambien pills, was rushed to the hospital. His stomach pumped out, he survived. Two weeks later he fell, broke his hip, contracted pneumonia in the hospital, and died.

Instead of attempting to talk Tim out of suicide, I should have been comforting, if not consorting with him in his wish to end his life.

When another friend of mine was dying of mesothelioma, it happened at the time that I was profoundly committed to formal Christian religious belief in afterlife. My friend was not. While he had sung regularly in his Episcopal church's choir, chanting at Easter the joy of Christ having risen, paradoxically he was convinced that no life existed after death. Yet in letters and discussion, I was attempting to convince him of the opposite. It was implausible for a person like myself, who swings periodically from belief to doubt, to be engaging in such discussion with a dying person. Nonetheless, I wrote him a letter.

"As with Mark Twain, predictions of your death are premature. There's life where there's hope.

"It was suggested that we might visit and have a glass of wine with you, but if you're not feeling up to it, I perfectly understand. You're on a journey, to be interrupted only at your wish.

"'We know what we are,' saith Hamlet, 'but know not what we may be.' The reason for our existence is clouded in mystery. Logic is a pathetic instrument to understand it. Perhaps your recent near-death experiences have at least suggested that you are on an exciting, even exotic journey that will take you to where you will be separated from your miserable, suffering body. Amazingly, there will be joy!

"You have been harshly realistic about the inevitability of a cancer-ridden death. No 'Onward, Christian Soldiers' for you. Nor me. But if Christ's divinity and the message of his crucifixion don't command your faith, you may at least be willing to admit that you've been a pretty good Christian . . . better than I. It's just that life slides along better with a faith proven of two thousand years, which has withstood Communism, fascism, utopianism, Freudian analysis, and every other *ism* that has ultimately failed.

"Enough of my sermonizing. If I don't see you, farewell."

I did get to see my friend a week or so before he died, and discovered that my letter had not gone down well with him. He remained firm in his belief that he was not going on a journey to anywhere. Death was the end, dammit, and no more talk of it being otherwise.

When I came to write this chapter, I realized that I needed superior information to help friends and relatives in their dying, so I enrolled in a local program training hospice volunteers. Hospice is defined as care for people whom doctors have given six months or less to live. Here was an opportunity for me to learn. The prolongation of old age has created a need for millions of workers adept at tending to people nearing their end. Skilled caretakers will be in short supply, unable to keep up with the soaring population 65 years and older, which is doubling in number between 2000 and 2030. Nowhere near meeting demand are nurses and nurse practitioners skilled in palliative care. More and more of the burden will fall on family members and volunteers.

Notwithstanding my age, the nearby Visiting Nurses Association found me capable of volunteer work. This VNA is owned by a giant health-care company, whose professionals perform most of the hospice work. To have its work subsidized by Medicare, the company must have five percent of it done by volunteers. I would train to be one of them, though not before I'd signed multiple forms related to confidentiality, behavior, and health. My blood was tested to make sure I wasn't a druggie.

Perhaps it should have been unsurprising that our instructor for the day was not a nurse, but a lawyer and former prosecuting attorney, a middle-aged woman, personable, good-looking, wearing cleanly pressed dark-grey pants, a pale-blue vest over a white blouse, her hair

RESPECTING A DYING PERSON'S WISHES

What if you're pressed to go into an assisted-living facility? What are the conditions under which you wish to be kept alive? Where do you want to be at the moment of dying, and with whom? What kind of memorial or funeral service do you want? Answer these questions in writing while you still are thinking clearly. An excellent guide to gaining better control of how you are treated when suffering terminal illness, and after you've died, is the pamphlet *Five Wishes*, which can be purchased by phoning 888.594.7437. It contains the prompts needed to give specific written advice to your family.

looking like it had been freshly coiffed a few hours ago. Facing her were three women and two men—novices in the art of caring for the terminally ill. We discovered that all of us had been involved in attending to the needs of friends and family members during their dying weeks. Now we were seated around a conference table in a cramped, soulless room on the fifth floor of a suburban New York office building, studying how to do it better.

Two of the women, like me, worked in publishing. The man, with harshly wrinkled facial skin and a wide, flat forehead, had the overall build of an athlete. "Yeah, I play baseball," he admitted, then added, "I recently lost my wife." His downcast eyes indicated he was still suffering the loss. Maybe volunteer hospice work would revitalize him.

For an hour we'd been poring through the contents of a two-hundred-page looseleaf binder on hospice care. Thirty color tabs marked different ways to listen to and communicate with people diagnosed as certain to die within the next six months. How should we converse successfully with a stranger nearing the end? With someone from a culture we don't know? With someone suffering the early stages of dementia? With a friend whose only wish is to die?

"We have another three and a half hours before we're finished," cautioned the instructor. "Take a break."

Glancing through the looseleaf binder, I began to realize that, in fact, I was largely void of real skills in communicating with someone who knows that they'll die soon. Choosing the wrong words in speaking to a sufferer is only one source of error, I learned. A slight voice inflection, or unwanted touching, or an inability to maintain eye contact, can be wrong. So too can be lack of empathy, or an excess of it. Or failing to see how things look to the dying person. In the case of Tim Tung, I should not have repeatedly tried to convince him not to commit suicide. I should have behaved more sympathetically, employing the words in hospice care book, "I can imagine how you feel. I wish it could happen for you. Tell me more."

Coffee break ended, we settled in our chairs, and resumed listening to the instructor. "If you realize that you've said something to a patient that is upsetting or inappropriate, immediately say to them, 'I didn't phrase that right.' Or, say, 'I'm sorry. I was clumsy with my words. I just want to say that I care about you, and don't want you to be alone in your suffering.' Remain authentic. If the patient has lost her hair, don't try to make her feel better by saying 'how lovely you look today.' She knows it's a lie.

"Turn to page 102 in your looseleaf binder," our instructor continued. "If the sufferer says, 'I'm dying,' don't falsely deny it. Rather say, 'Tell me about that. Let's discuss it. What's your understanding of what the doctors say? What are you hoping for?' Focus on short-term goals, and how you can help him or her achieve them. Expand the conversation.

"You may hear the expression, 'I feel my life has been a failure.' Don't immediately jump in and respond, 'Oh no!' Rather say, 'Tell me more about that. Let's think back in time.' With luck the conversation will turn to positive accomplishments achieved by the person during his or her life, good deeds that had been forgotten.

"Avoid the words, '*You should*.' Discover and orient patients to whatever they have in their own spiritual toolbox. Avoid jumping in and offering advice to solve a problem they've just described. Wait to be invited to talk. And avoid being judgmental."

Her eyes accidentally turned to someone in the room who'd spent his professional life making a living from judging. It's what editors do. I would have to suppress a natural form of behavior.

"Suppose the person is suffering dementia?" I asked.

"Agree with the person's reality, don't judge. If you're with a patient suffering mild dementia, and in his delusion he says, 'I'm having breakfast tomorrow with my cousin who's in Ohio,' don't correct him. Don't argue. Respond by saying, 'Interesting. What does your cousin do? How old is he? Tell me about him.'

"What should you do," she continued, "if you sense the patient and caretaker, or the patient and family are arguing with one another? Look in your binder. It's covered in the section called Complex Family Dynamics." She paused, looking expectantly at us. "Any questions?"

"Recently," I said, "I read about something called Reminiscence Therapy. It started in Holland in an assisted living facility where residents with Alzheimer's and cognitive disorders were made to feel better."

"Yes, I've heard of it," the instructor said. "Tell us."

"It seems that people form their strongest memories between the ages of ten and thirty. So if we're talking now to someone who's eighty-five years old, their strongest memories are from the period between 1945 and 1965.

"I remember the time well. It should make it easy for me to have verbal exchanges with octogenarians suffering severe memory loss and frustration from it, or with friends of my age facing the end. We can reminiscence about what was happening in our lives during our teens and twenties. Like necking in the car at outdoor movies, zoot suits, Eisenhower and the McCarthy hearings on TV, the meager two or three times a year we enjoyed a full-menu dinner in a restaurant."

"Whatever works," observed one of the women at the table. "My problem is that while I feel compassion, I can't find the words to articulate my sympathy. I feel awkward trying to express a feeling for the patient who's undergoing something that I've never experienced."

"Don't fret," said the instructor. "Be comfortable with silence. Just sitting with the person can be a gift to them. Your quiet presence may be all they need to assuage their suffering."

Words aren't the only effective means of communicating with people over whom death hovers. Much of an hour spent with the dying person can involve light massage, or music. A physician, an accomplished violinist, lay dying in a hospital's ICU. He had mistakenly been given a medication to which he was discovered to be highly allergic. Less than a couple of hours away from dying, his wife had the idea of wiring the earphones from her iPhone into his ears so that he would pass out of this life hearing his favorite music, Bach's *St. Matthew's Passion.*

Slowly the man came back to life. Two days later he was released from the hospital.

In our village, my friend Judy Hill told me of how she was able to help a Guatemalan guy who spoke no English. She didn't speak to him at all. She massaged his feet, applying a spiritually guided life-force called Energy Reiki. His wife told Judy that her wordless visit was the best he'd ever had.

When she was aiding a dying woman in her nineties, Judy discovered that the woman had fallen behind in sending Christmas cards to her grandchildren. "So I helped her write, address and mail cards. 'There's one grandchild I don't want to send a card to,' she told me. 'She's in prison, serving a sentence for drug dealing. She's a huge disappointment.'

"I talked with the woman about the rewards of forgiveness," said Judy. "The next day she resolved, after all, to send her granddaughter a Christmas card. Two weeks later she received a letter bearing the postmark of the correctional facility where the girl was incarcerated. The granddaughter wrote about the happiness and relief that she felt. How much she regretted her crime. How important her grand-mother's love was. And so it brought peace and happiness to the grandmother, and not long afterwards she died happily.

"The moral is to get complete with relationships," Judy said.

"Don't leave anything hanging. Don't let death happen and miss the chance to forgive, commune, confess. When my husband was near dying of cancer we made a date to say goodbye. We made notes to prepare ourselves to talk. We lit candles. We had a cocktail at hand. We said what we had to say. Within a week he died.

"So many I've nursed in hospice are frightened at the prospect of death," added Judy. "They cling to life, fight to the end. They fear their sins will never be forgiven. They believe there's a heaven and hell, that there's a punishing God, that they haven't lived up to the standards of their religion. 'Don't take me,' they plead."

The British writer Aldous Huxley, author of *Brave New World* and *The Doors of Perception*, told of how he was able to ease his wife Maria through her final days in 1955 at their home in California. How he did it can be found in Appendix 3 of the extraordinary book *Psychedelic Prophets*, Huxley's correspondence with his dear friend Humphry Osmond (Chapter 10). In the sidebar to this chapter is a digest of what Huxley wrote.

After Maria died, Osmond wrote Huxley a letter of praise for the graceful manner in which he had eased his wife on the way to her end. Dying, wrote Osmond, is just a way across the border, an easing of the strands that bind to this world. On the day Huxley himself died in 1963, only hours after President Kennedy's assassination, he received LSD so that he could trip to another world, the one resembling the hallucinogenic one he had always believed was more valid than our everyday experience.

People face death in a variety of ways—gracefully, angrily, gratefully, spiritually, even humorously. To achieve even modest success, the caretaker has to avoid being judgmental. To help someone make the journey into dying, it's necessary to recognize that the paths are as varied as those of living.

HOW ALDOUS HUXLEY COMFORTED HIS WIFE AS SHE WAS DYING

I spent a good many hours of each day sitting with her, sometimes saying nothing. When I spoke . . . I would go through the procedure of hypnotic induction, beginning by suggestions of muscular relaxation, then counting to five or ten, with the suggestion at each count to send her deeper into hypnosis. I would accompany the counting with passes of the hand, which I drew slowly down from the head towards the feet.

(Maria Huxley passionately loved the desert, where she had experienced visionary and mystical experiences associated with light.)

I would begin by reminding her of the desert she had loved so much, of the vast crystalline silence, of the overarching sky. I would ask her to open her eyes to the memory of the desert sky, and to think of it as the blue light of Peace, soft and yet intense, gentle and yet irresistible in its tranquilizing power. In the South rose the mountains, covered with snow and glowing with the white light of pure Being . . . of which love, joy, and peace are manifestations and in which all the dualisms of our experience, all the pairs of opposites—positive and negative, good and evil, pleasure and pain, health and sickness, life and death—are reconciled and made one . . . And I kept on repeating this, urging her to go deeper and deeper into the light.

So the days passed and, as her body weakened, her surface mind drifted further and further out of contact . . . At a little before three on Saturday morning, the night nurse came to tell us that her pulse was failing.

I went and sat by Maria's bed, leaned over and spoke into her ear. I told her that I was with her and would always be with her in that light which is the central reality of our beings. I told her to let go, to forget the body, to leave it lying there like a bundle of old clothes, and to allow herself to be carried, as a child is carried, into the heart of the rosy light of love . . . Now she must go forward into love, deeper and deeper, so that at last she would be capable of loving as God loves—of loving everything, infinitely, without judging, without condemning, without either craving or abhorring.

For the last hour I sat or stood with my left hand on her head and the right on the solar plexus. Between two right-handed persons this contact seems to create a kind of vital circuit . . . The breathing became quieter.

I went on with my suggestions and reminders, repeating them close to her ear, 'Let go, let go. Forget the body, leave it lying here. It is of no importance now . . . Only the light. Only this peace.' When the breathing ceased about six, it was without any struggle.

This text is excised and reprinted with permission of the Aldous and Laura Huxley Literary Trust

CHAPTER 16

IN MEMORIAM

The moving finger writes; and, having writ
Moves on; nor all thy piety nor wit
Shall lure it back to cancel half a line,
Nor all thy tears wash out a word of it.
Edward Fitzgerald, "The Rubáiyát of Omar Khayyám"

The internet is littered with links to books, blogs and websites offering advice on how to conduct a service memorializing the one who cannot return, whose life, not half a line of it, can't be erased. Enter the words "plan memorial funeral" on Google, and a click will take you to an interminable list of tips, including *34 Unique Memorial Service Ideas Urns Online.* You will be inundated with advice on how to create a memorable event. Also available in cyberspace are boilerplate obituaries. Fill in the blanks with facts about your own dearly beloved. No need to inflict bad writing on friends, it's available online.

With so much free and seemingly well-informed advice available, why so many unwritten obituaries, or badly composed ones? Why so many memorial services gone wrong? This chapter dishes up a few dumbfounding examples—a distillation of what I've learned from a forgotten number of memorial services and funerals that I've attended, and of dozens of obituaries I've written.

A family member has just died. After phoning 911 or the funeral home, the decent thing to do is to tell the deceased's closest friends what has happened. Remarkably, this often doesn't happen. It fails to occur to many children that their parents actually had friends, even though a bulging Rolodex next to the kitchen phone suggests their existence. Or that the Dell computer in the study upstairs contains the email addresses of most of the people who would want to know that your mom just died and that she specifically requested sushi not be served at the wake.

The next important act is to provide an obituary for the local paper, for the college alumni magazine, and maybe buy the space for one in *The New York Times*. The compilation of the biographical facts needed to compose an obituary should have been done by the dearly departed in the time available to him between rounds of golf and bridge. Sad to say, he failed to do so, along with failing to record what family member should inherit his Picasso first-edition print, his timeshare in Boca Raton, and the rowboat on Lake Begone.

An obituary's first couple of sentences is the key to attracting attention. What was the deceased's principal life achievement? I found the question answered in all six of the obituaries written by professional journalists in a recent issue of *The New York Times*. Of the twenty paid obituaries in the same issue, written by amateurs, only three began by citing the dead person's most significant accomplishments.

"Margaret Jones, wife of the late John Jones, passed away on June 9 at her home in Palm Beach after a long battle with cancer." Several paragraphs later, the reader learns what should have been in the first paragraph: "Margaret Jones, a precocious violinist, who at age 21 played in the New York Philharmonic orchestra conducted by Leonard Bernstein, died on June 9."

What if the deceased failed to do or to invent something that would make his or her obituary more compelling? No problem. All he or she needs to have done is to have participated enthusiastically in improving an aspect of daily living. Let's say he was a pretty good card player. "Over 40 years the game of poker wheeled into Edward's gas station where its tank was filled with his super-octane energy."

Of Journalism 101's five Ws and one H—who, what, where, when, why, how—the most important words spoken at a memorial service, again, are the dead person's notable accomplishments. The information should be front and center. Often, though, the deceased's wondrous deeds emerge twenty minutes into a speech given by a relative who never before has made a public oration. Or it is lost in the broken whispered tearful recollection of a daughter who sobs so uncontrollably that her words can't be understood.

At a hotel ballroom memorial for a publishing colleague, at which I was to be the second of four speakers, the widow had selected the deceased's brother to lead off the talks. It seemed not to have occurred to the guy that the anecdotes and incidents in his life were insignificant and inconsequential for the 75 or so people gathered in the hotel public space. As they stared down at their half-eaten chicken salads and drained wine glasses, he spoke for 45 minutes, reminiscing more about himself than about his recently departed sibling. The energy in the room fizzled like the air from a punctured balloon.

Anyone who finds they're in charge of organizing a memorial service—it's usually a surviving spouse—should not shirk from the ruthlessness required to tell speakers forcefully that their time is limited to five minutes, or whatever span of time is appropriate given the number of speakers. Here's an interesting if insensitive idea: place ashes of the deceased in a five-minute glass timer to remind the speaker of when to complete their reminiscences.

Review with each speaker what he or she is going to say so that stories and facts aren't repeated. The late-lamented was a multifaceted person, who not only may have been responsible for a couple of outstanding material achievements, but who may have possessed a few charming or not-so-charming habits, including compassion, a contagious laugh, an easily aroused anger, extreme generosity, practical jokes, inexhaustible energy. In a well-planned memorial service, these characteristics are evoked by a succession of speakers without duplication.

The speakers need to be reminded to talk less about themselves, and mainly about the dearly departed. At a memorial at the Frank E. Campbell Funeral Chapel in Manhattan, the "funeral home to the stars" where former New York City Mayor Ed Koch's body lay downstairs awaiting burial, we were mourning the death of my friend Dr. John Higgins, a veterinarian favored by pet-owning millionaires, actors, and celebrities living on Manhattan's Upper East Side. The principal speaker was a photojournalist who, like me, was a friend of the deceased. For a quarter of an hour he read from a text about how his own life had been affected by events involving Higgins. The only thing largely missing from his talk was Higgins himself.

Every seat in the room was occupied by persons whose eyes, I observed, boredom had caused to glaze over. They must be admiring, loving dog-owners, I thought, here at the Campbell Funeral Chapel to recall the deftness with which the good doctor had healed a wounded paw or administered a rabies shot. It turned out they were all Alcoholics Anonymous members, who for years had helped the vet in his successful battle against the demon rum. AA members commonly attend the funerals of their fellow members. Notwithstanding the anonymity for which AA is noted, they sign the funeral register.

Old film and VCR recordings, maybe television interviews, are the raw material of a video that can surpass words in evoking the life of the deceased. Time and money to hire a professional director are needed to produce such a show for a memorial service, along with the tech needed to project on a large screen or multiple TV monitors. It works. During a recent memorial service, I heard laughter and crying as a hundred people watched images and heard words of my friend Olympic skier and resort founder Tom Corcoran, as if he were still with us.

A superior memorial service or funeral is one planned by yourself while you're still *compos mentis*. Failure to record your written desire will leave a spouse or child in charge. When they aren't comfortable organizing, or they lack confidence, the funeral home or the church pastor typically takes over.

After Walter Liedtke, the distinguished curator of Dutch and Flemish art at New York's Metropolitan Museum, died in a tragic train crash, his widow Nancy decided to hold his memorial service at St. Matthew's Episcopal Church in Bedford in northern Westchester County, a toney New York exurb.

The freshly painted, white interior of St. Matthew's is austere in its loveliness. The altar is plain and simple, the crucifix small and unimposing. The church's congregation is largely made up of haute-monde Bedford residents who have managed to evade the embraces of agnosticism or atheism.

The memorial service began as well as any I've ever attended. The recollections of his colleagues at the Metropolitan Museum were exquisitely spoken, intellectually rich. When the time came for the concluding eulogy, the Rector of St. Matthew's clearly had in mind that people renting his place for a memorial were going to hear the holy message, whether they liked it or not. He spoke glowingly of Walter in his new life in heaven above.

I was shocked. I also sensed a stirring in the pews among Walter's friends. Walter in heaven? Up there? It was not a place Walter himself believed to exist, except perhaps in visual form when he gazed at Rembrandt's painting of Christ's Ascension. The good reverend, though, had his day, even if his listeners staggered out into sunlight wondering what Walter would have thought of it all.

None of the foregoing advice, of course, is needed if a funeral or memorial does not take place. The deceased decided that's the way it should be. No fuss or bother over me, he told his wife and children. I want the world to remember, even admire me as a humble, unpretentious, modest, self-effacing person, who didn't require his family to spend a lot of money staging a memorial.

What appears to be selfless is arguably selfish. Barring a family from staging a memorial service may actually be a lack of empathy for friends who are deprived of enjoying the opportunity to celebrate the deceased's life. They were a popular character . . . loved for his or her accomplishments and generosity. It's a flawed decision not to gather in remembrance, sharing stories about times spent together.

After an old skiing friend died, I was asked to speak at his memorial service in Woodstock, on the eastern edge of New York's Catskill Mountains. The afternoon memorial took place in an art gallery. The service was not, and he was not, religious.

Most of my skiing with my friend had been here, in the Catskills, forty and more years earlier. Before I set out on the drive north, I noticed that snow was forecast, so I stuck my ski gear in the car, just in case . . . .

For those who think that life's end should be a solemn affair, the idea of planning a combined funeral and ski trip may seem frivolous, or outright disrespectful. But why should it be?

Following the memorial service I spent the night in a motel in the village of Fleischmanns, not far from the home of the inventor in 1952 of the revolutionary Cubco ski binding, and of Highmount, a lost ski area. Both gone.

In the morning I drove the dozen miles to the base of Belleayre Mountain. Six inches of fresh powder had fallen overnight. I was among the first lift riders. Like most skiers over the years, I can't find words to describe what happened next . . . two hours of ineffable, raw pleasure, cruising in snow lying light as feathers on a groomed base. Turns came effortlessly, the skis silent as they sliced the down-like snow.

It wasn't the day's only satisfaction. On the slope under the lift, blue and red poles were set for a giant slalom race. Volunteer gatekeepers were in position. I caught a chair ride with an eight-year-old girl, geared to compete.

"What's the race?" I asked.

"A mini-World Cup," she murmured. Dreams of Mikaela Shiffrin danced under the little helmet. But this petite racer had another concern. Her bib number was 7, and already bib number 1 was on the course. "When we unload," I urged her, "head straight for the starting gate. Don't worry. You'll make it!" She did.

I watched as parents herded their kids, issuing the ages-old warning not to speed out of control. On stubby skis and snowboards they struggled or soared. All over the mountain children and parents exulted in the brilliance of sunlight and pristine whiteness. Their shouts of happiness rang across the slopes. Skiing was alive and well, recycling its history, the conqueror of time otherwise wasted. That Sunday I found myself celebrating my friend's life more than mourning his death.

Memorial orations occasionally inspire, even bring new action into your life. The priest officiating at the funeral of my first wife—she was a writer and English professor—urged friends and former students gathered around the grave to focus on the spiritual space she had found, a source of beauty and truth and light.

"I want to urge you to give yourselves a gift from Ann," urged the priest. "Become intentional about pressing into this space." The impact of his message could be seen in the eyes and faces of people as they walked away from the outdoor service to their cars.

Before my friend and school psychologist Jim Terleph died of the excruciating Lou Gehrig disease, ALS, he wrote something that he asked his widow Ann to speak at his memorial service. The couple had throughout their lives been inveterate travelers.

Ann, in a crisp Oxonian British voice that rang clear as a bell in the hushed church, pronounced her husband's words.

"Not long after I received the diagnosis that eventually killed me, I was asked if Ann and I were planning any more travel. Thinking for a second, I said 'No,' though like Hamlet I would be going to 'that undiscovered country from whose bourn no traveler returns.'

"As one who always loved to travel, I thought about it some more. It will not be so bad really, I reflected. After all, you don't need a visa, or even a passport. No worrying about transportation. You don't have to bother about reservations at your destination. You don't have to be concerned about the amount of money needed, immunizations, or the right clothes to take. Even though it might be one's last trip, in a way it's an ideal one. Though many people have gone there, since they never reported on it, you will get to see something really unusual."

Tears—triggered by sadness and laughter—moistened the eyes and cheeks of the hundred or so friends and relatives who'd come to the service. It was a memorial to remember.

CHAPTER 17

AN ODDITY OF GRIEF

He is my other eyes that can see above the clouds;
my other ears that hear above the winds.
When I am wrong, he is delighted to forgive.
When I am angry, he clowns to make me smile.

"He's Just My Dog," Gene Hill

As fresh news arrives, almost weekly, about the death of another close friend or near-relative, I'm suffused with numbness. Why am I not burning with grief? Do I lack compassion? Am I freezing my emotions as a way to anesthetize myself against the pain of the loss? Do I lack the courage to cope with anguish?

An emotional quotient seems to be missing. I feel guilt. No tears slither down my cheeks. In confessing this vacant state of mind to a couple of ninety-year-old friends, I've discovered that I'm not alone in my emotional apathy on hearing about the demise of dear friends. As an escape, we reminisce about good times spent together with the deceased, maybe an argument we once had and both forgave. We are so regularly bombarded with news of deaths that we become shell-shocked, numb. Absent is the empathy that was also missing in me when I stood at my father's bedside as he was dying, described in Chapter 15.

What makes it worse is that I know what it's like to mourn in the most piercing way. It raises ironic, if not profound, questions about what it means to grieve: how much fiercer and penetrating it can be, how strange, to suffer more from the death of an animal than of a human.

In 2008 my ten-year-old cairn terrier grabbed a lamb chop, and tried to swallow it whole. The chop became fixed in Geordie's throat. He had been unable to eat solid food now for days, and was wasting away. The surgery that would be involved in removing the splintered piece of bone, advised the veterinarian, would permanently impair the dog's ability to eat normally. The only option was to put Geordie down. Euthanize him.

We reluctantly agreed. Leading the dog on his leash, my wife and I were ushered into a private room to spend with Geordie the final minutes of his life.

I raised him onto the examination table. We watched as the vet injected the lethal dose into the dog's thigh.

Now my wife held Geordie in her arms. I placed my hand on his neck to comfort him. He looked at me with innocent eyes, seeking assurance that all would be well, that surely I must know what the hell I'm doing. In a little more than a minute he was motionless, his jaw slightly open, the tongue lifeless.

Instantly I felt pressure surge from my lungs into my nostrils and my eyes. My mouth popped open. Involuntarily I began to sob. I bent over, convulsed. Tears fell to the floor. Here was an experience remotely different from the reaction I felt when my mother, father, and sister had died.

Why we grieve more outwardly the death of a pet than that of a human is typically explained this way. Our relationships with family members and friends are unfathomably complex, filled with love and argument, loyalty and betrayal, logic and illogic, accord and misunderstanding, forgiveness and resentment, faith and faithlessness, relationships with others.

Our relationship to our pet, by contrast, is simple. We don't argue. Neither of us is disloyal. We instantly forgive or forget a transgression.

"A dog is the only animal whose emotions we can truly penetrate," wrote British book editor and author Diana Athill in *Somewhere toward the End*, her perspective on aging. "Dogs and humans recognize each other at a deep and uncomplicated level. When a dog is anxious, angry, hungry, puzzled, happy, loving, it allows us to see in purest form states which we ourselves know, though in us distorted by the complex accretions of humanity."

The relationship is somewhat one-sided. In return for supplying food and shelter, we get obedience through training, and we receive an unmitigated flow of love. We experience in the dog's eyes the innocence and trust found in the eyes of a two-year-old child. It goes to our hearts.

While it may go figuratively to our hearts, it actually goes physically through a part of our body between the brainstem and the cortex, known as the caudate nucleus. Both humans and dogs have caudates. According to the neuroeconomics professor Gregory Burns, the caudate, which is rich in dopamine receptors, induces positive emotions when activated like love and attachment. Dogs thus have a level of sentience comparable to that of a human child, according to Dr. Burns. Perhaps even more. A dog's shameless affection is not limited to people. Not forgetting that a dog's best friend is another dog, not a man, a dog can also be the best friend of a cat, a sheep, or a goat.

Dogs have a unique capacity for interspecies love, according to Dr. Clive Wynne, a psychologist at Arizona State University, who specializes in dog behavior. Dogs, he says, have "an abnormal willingness to form strong emotional bonds with almost anything that crosses their path." Among his discoveries is that the part of a dog's brain which lights up when hearing its owner's voice is the same part of the human brain which lights up when we are fond of someone or something.

It also helps that, in their evolution and breeding, dogs have developed a small brow muscle that makes their eyes look larger, infant-like, appealingly innocent, impossible for us not to respond sympathetically. If such a muscle exists in humans it must have atrophied in most of us some time after infancy.

In a way, we contrive a dog's entire life. We go to a breeder of golden retrievers or Australian shepherds or cairn terriers and order a puppy from a litter not yet born. Our future pet's mother is bred, we bring the four-month-old puppy home. Ten or fifteen years later when the dog is infirm, we decide that it's time for our beloved to die. What we brought to life, we end. We order the death of the one we love, and who loved us. The experience is so shocking, we are so ill-equipped to deal emotionally with it, that it leads to the most acutely felt grief.

"When I have lost a dog," said the actress Mary Tyler Moore, "I have gone into a mourning period that lasted for months."

The author V.S. Naipaul did not find it odd to compare the grief he felt over the death of his father and brother to that he felt for his cat, which he found almost more profound and tangible.

The grief may last a few months . . . not the years that characterizes the loss of a dear friend. Replacing a lost spouse is even more difficult or impossible. Stuck, the widow or widower needs to avoid getting depressed, and move forward. How to overcome such grief? The answers exist in countless books, and in a flood of advice on the internet. Or you can get a dog.

And live longer. Compared with people who don't own a dog, people who do have a twenty-four percent lower risk of dying at any age, especially from a heart attack, according to research involving hundreds of thousands of people. The reason is simple. Owners of dogs walk regularly, they are less isolated socially, and are less depressed because they feel loved and adored. With them we go gentle into that good night.

CHAPTER 18

LIFE AFTER DEATH?

Strange, is it not? that of the myriads who
Before us passed the door of darkness through,
Not one returns to tell us of the road,
Which to discover we must travel too.
Edward Fitzgerald, "The Rubáiyát of Omar Khayyám"

My life closed twice before its close
It yet remains to see
If Immortality unveil
A third event to me
Emily Dickinson

The question haunts us, whether we like it or not: Is there life after death? Will you exist in some form after dying? Is your real prospect literally *dust to dust*? Is there a Christian or Islamic afterlife where the potential exists to wind up, if not in Heaven, in an incendiary Hell? Or an Eastern belief that we return to the world in another form?

Of course, you can be indifferent to such questions, as I am not. If you don't care, you're probably not reading this book.

Even if you don't believe there's a postmortem existence awaiting us, you're forced to contend with the factual evidence that some kind of life exists in a nonphysical world. Not biology, bread, or water are needed for consciousness to exist. The fact has been proven over and over in phenomena such as extrasensory perception, the experiences of people who have clinically died and returned to life, in the ability of mediums to be in contact with persons long dead, scientifically and carefully scrutinized to ensure the absence of fraud.

The existence of afterlife no longer derives from religious or cult belief. The evidence for its possibility is overwhelming. Hundreds of carefully documented cases of people describe a domain which they inhabited while they were clinically dead with no brain function. There are numerous cases of toddlers who describe in factually accurate detail their previous existence as another person.

"People often ask me if I believe in life after death," says Peter Fenwick, a British neuropsychiatrist with over two hundred published papers on brain function. "I always say that it is no longer a question of belief. This question must be removed from field of belief into the field of data."

The journalist Leslie Kean, drawing on her own reporting and from the expertise of neuroscientists, writes that even if the definite existence of consciousness, separate from the physical, is impossible to prove scientifically, the factual evidence for it is ample. The phenomenon of extrasensory perception—telepathy, clairvoyance, psychokinesis, precognition—may be controversial, but ESP has been documented by legitimate scientists for many years. We see it in people communicating to us from another world long after they've died, or briefly visited by thousands of people when they nearly died.

"Human beings have extraordinary mental abilities that science cannot explain." says Kean in her book *Surviving Death*. Just as science does not yet understand dark energy, which makes up about three quarters of our universe, within our interior universe science doesn't understand the nature of consciousness either.

Perhaps the closest we have come yet to understanding consciousness is its similarity to the nonlocality of subatomic particles. In the physics of nonlocality, objects instantaneously know about each other's state, even when separated by large distances of millions of light years. Similarly, consciousness cannot be located in a particular time and place.

Instead of science being the enemy of religion, as it was perceived during the Age of Reason, contemporary science is coming to recognize its own limits. There may be phenomena we will never know. We are being led back to the awe and timeless mystery of our existence.

In Western culture the belief in postmortem life primarily finds its inspiration in the New Testament accounts of Christ's resurrection. Every Sunday millions of churchgoers dutifully recite the Nicene Creed, agreeing that a man's body was physically conveyed to God's right-hand side. Worshippers are told He died for our sins. I also happen to think that Christ, condemned to torturous execution by a Roman governor and theocrats, did it—not for forgiveness of our sins—but partly to remind us of the dangers of uniting organized religion with government, by the example of Pontius Pilate's collusion with the Sanhedrin.

I was forced to memorize the Nicene Creed at age fourteen so as to be confirmed in the Anglican Church. The experience of Confirmation instruction was so boring and stultifying that it led me to agnosticism. For another fifty years I flitted in and out of a crowd labeled by the Catholic nighttime TV comedian Stephen Colbert as "atheists without balls."

Then came a revelation of sorts. As I was researching my book *The Story of Modern Skiing*, published by University Press of New England in 2006, I became immersed in studying the remarkable life of Sir Arnold Lunn, an important figure in the early history of skiing and mountain climbing—sports about which I've written tens of thousands of words. Lunn is most famous for his 1924 invention of the modern timed slalom race. As well, he led the campaign that eventually brought alpine ski racing into the Olympics in 1936. In 1952, a kneeling Lunn was among the first persons to be knighted by the newly crowned Queen Elizabeth.

Lunn wrote as many books—two dozen—about philosophy and religion as he did about skiing and mountaineering. Odd indeed was a man who in the morning could write an essay recalling a snowy alpine ski descent, and in the afternoon turn his mind to proving the bodily ascension to heaven of a Jewish heretic crucified by the Roman occupiers of Israel two thousand years earlier. Lunn wrote an entire book, *The Third Day*, seeking to prove, as an historical event, that Christ, after entombment, reappeared, then rose to sit on the right-hand side of you-know-who.

I came to parse in the pages of *Commonweal* and *The Tablet* magazines how Lunn intertwined mountaineering and religion in his life. I was also encouraged to write his biography by the archivist at Georgetown University where his voluminous papers reside. I regret not undertaking the work. I wished that I'd known the guy—not just his words on paper. Lunn was witty, stupendously educated, a brilliant orator at Oxford when he was a student there. He would have been fun to be with.

"With his energetic, derisive, iconoclastic mind and rasping demonic laugh," wrote the literary critic A.J. Ackerley, "Lunn was both the vitality and terror of the community."

Author and *Firing Line* TV host William F. Buckley adored

Arnold Lunn, annually skiing with him in the Bernese Oberland. The two were fervent adherents of Roman Catholicism, Buckley born to it, Lunn a convert. In his book *Nearer My God*, Buckley cribbed some of his ideas on Christ's resurrection from Lunn's *The Third Day*.

With Arthur Conan Doyle, Lunn was an enthusiastic participant in séances, and partial materialization telekinesis. Countless verified accounts of people in touch with the dead reinforced Lunn's belief in postmortem existence experiences. One of the most popular cases trotted out by afterlife believers is that of the mathematician and philosopher Bertrand Russell. While alive, Russell was a vehement skeptic. He insisted that after dying his body would rot and his ego would vanish. Yet four years after his demise in 1970, Russell—from some extraterritorial place—lucidly described to the medium Rosemary Brown what life was like now that he was dead.

After his 1932 conversion to Catholicism, Lunn retreated from his belief in the authenticity of the extraterrestrial voices he'd once heard. Conan Doyle never did, but remained a friend.

Definitely unconvinced that neither one's soul nor one's body can survive physical death was Lunn's contemporary, the masterful British fiction writer W. Somerset Maugham, an avid atheist. It's said that Maugham, as he lay dying at his home on the French Riviera in 1965, desperately wanted assurance of his belief that there would be no future existence for him in the beyond. He arranged for the renowned logical positivist philosopher A. J. Ayer to fly from England to his home on the Mediterranean. There, Ayer, the world's most logical man, like a priest delivering last rites, would assure Maugham of his postmortem nonexistence.

The philosopher dutifully delivered at the famous author's bedside the godless words of consolation that the dying man longed to hear. Maugham might better have occupied his intellect in writing a story about an old author who, moments before his death, recognizes that logic cannot prove there's no life after death. Only belief can.

Lunn also believed in the miraculous cures experienced by the lame and sick who went to Lourdes. He was on board with St. Augustine, who wrote, "Miracles are not contrary to nature, but only contrary to what we know about nature." The miracle of Christ's bodily resurrection is partly rooted in a Biblically rooted reward system: the volume of goodness in one's terrestrial life favors the odds of gaining admission to a heavenly one.

Today, in church on Sunday, pew-occupiers typically doubt the words of the Nicene Creed averring Christ's Resurrection. It's a total muddle to think of God as possessing either a right or a left side, for example. Priests are left to deal with parishioners' doubts about the virginity of Mary. Regarding Christ's Resurrection, most often they tell the Sunday service attendee that it's not necessarily heretical to interpret the Ascension as a spiritual, noncorporal event. Mind—not matter, as painted by Rembrandt and Giotto—rose to heaven. No Savior is needed, no Church required.

Today, four out of five Americans believe in an afterlife—among them, Milennials, said to be the least-religious generation in American history. They have rapidly grown in number. Why the increased belief in an afterlife over a period when church attendance is plummeting? The idea arises in young people, not from religious conviction, but from the paranormal in movies and television, and from stories of near-death experiences. Add to that the fact that three of every ten Americans believe in astrology, according to a Pew Research poll.

The poet Christian Wiman, in his scintillating spiritual exploration *My Bright Abyss*, writes that Christ is not alive now because he rose from the dead two thousand years ago. "He rose from the dead two thousand years ago because he is alive right now" in the minds and spirits of millions.

Or why should we be arguing at all about whether there's an afterlife? Aldous Huxley in his *The Doors of Perception* wrote about a world accessed by mystics, mediums, and in his case by ingesting mescalin, assisted by Humphry Osmond whom we encountered in Chapter 10. There exists a fantastical, spiritual world out there that we don't tune into in our regular consciousness, and that is unrecognized by conventional scientific method.

The philosopher Ervin Laszlo postulates a universe pervaded by consciousness. It exists even when we don't. Our brain is a kind of TV set, displaying in us one spectrum of a universal consciousness that's out there. It continues to exist after our brain is physically dead. Turning off the TV set doesn't turn off the program. Dying doesn't end mind-life.

"If quantum entanglement is true," speculates poet/philosopher Wiman, "if related particles react in similar or opposite ways even when separated by tremendous distances, then it is obvious that the whole world is alive and communicating in ways we do not fully understand. We are part of the communication even as our atoms begin the long dispersal we call death."

I recently wrote my own words poetizing my notion of ultimacy.

There is a place where you may go,
I perhaps
and you with your faith-filled hope.
Where time does not have to be invented
We will see the real.
There is a place where we may go
Where protons oscillate and flow,
and know one another across interminable spaces.
The particles that will be you
gone to a universal place.
I, with you.

CHAPTER 19

FACING THE END

We are obliged by the deepest drives of the human spirit to make ourselves more than animated dust, and we must have a story to tell about where we came from, and why we are here.

E.O. Wilson

Socrates had it wrong; it is not the unexamined but the uncommitted life that is not worth living.

William Sloane Coffin

*My God my bright abyss
into which all my longing will not go
once more I come to the edge of all I know
and believing nothing believe in this.*

Christian Wiman

After near-fatal mountain accidents, shipwreck, not getting eaten by a bear, and NDE, I will likely die, as many of us do, attached to wires in a hospital intensive-care unit, or alone in the antiseptic nursing wing of an assisted-living residence. Each day the defenses crumble. An illness takes weeks, not days, to recover from. Observing myself in a mirror I see a face vaguely resembling a George Grosz caricature.

I have completed a standard living will that hopefully will prevent doctors from keeping me alive if there's certainty of my imminent death. Like most people, I fear the physical pain that I will likely suffer. At a juncture where I am unable to run or climb, suffer agonizing constipation, vision blurred, hearing faint, body frail, joints aching with arthritis, death, instead of terrifying, will be a grateful act of surrender. At ninety, certain that maybe a half-dozen years lie ahead, I am afraid not of death, but of the *godawful* process of dying. The end itself will be welcome. The certitude that maybe only a half-dozen years are left, accompanied by a satisfaction with one's life, is utterly different from the experience of a forty-five-year-old, suffering a cancer that will cause him to die, observing me and forty-five years of living he won't enjoy.

It would help to get through the experience at the end if one would have found the answer to why one existed, or what was the meaning of one's life. In that regard, I will die foiled, notwithstanding the reading of how-to books counseling us on how to encounter the prospect of death, starting with Plato's *Apology of Socrates*.

All the ideation that I've cultivated is beginning to look like an intellectual veneer that will be stripped away in the agony of dying. I will die as ordinarily as I've lived—protesting the damned injustice of it, criticizing the hospital staff, demanding more morphine or Demerol to extinguish the pain.

No, that is not it. The mere pursuit of philosophical study, even if it has produced no convincing teleological conclusion in my mind, has equipped me to face the prospect of death with lessened fear or anxiety. My friend Lou Marinoff, an alum of the private boys' school that I attended in Montreal, agrees with me. Lou has built a cottage industry around the idea that philosophy can be as good as Freudian analysis in combating neurosis and anxiety. His book *Plato, Not Prozac!* has sold two million copies and has been translated into twenty languages.

I still garden, play golf, hike and ski, and consider my life to have been lucky. But it makes me poorly equipped to advise less lucky people, whose lives have been damaged by prolonged illness, abusive parents, lack of education, extreme poverty, and tragedies. I'm reminded of what Diana Athill writes in her memoir *Somewhere Towards the End*. Athill, who had led a lucky life, thought herself inadequate in addressing people who'd not. "Whatever is said about old age by a luckier person such as I am is likely to be meaningless, or even offensive."

The poet and fiction writer Raymond Carver, as he was dying of cancer, wrote these lines:

And did you get what
you wanted from this life, even so?
I did.
And what did you want?
To call myself beloved, to feel myself
beloved on the earth.

A common reason people die depressed and unhappy is their belief that their lives have lacked value. What was missing? Beyond everyday existence, what is it they should have confronted? They didn't find the time to seek the answer. Day in, day out, they were engaged in mundane tasks and worries, combating boredom, living in a minimally reflective way.

The Danish philosopher Soren Kierkegaard, whose ideas capsized me (Chapters 5, 12), wrote about what he conceived as the lowest level of existence. He called it "the aesthetic level." Like most everyone, I live parts of my life in its daily grip. Kierkegaard regarded it as a sickness.

"To be a normal cultural man is, for Kierkegaard, to be sick, whether one knows it or not," wrote Ernest Becker in his 1973 Pulitzer Prize-winning *Denial of Death*. Modern men and women are engaged in day-to-day shopping, Web-based social media, and drugs that deprive them of a wider and deeper awareness. Its absence can be combated by exercises in nonjudging mindfulness, transcendental meditation, or joining in spiritual discourse with others. To combat spiritual malnutrition, my idea of bliss is to lie on my back in the grass, and put on a recording of Judy Collins singing "Amazing Grace." I stare into the star-filled night wondering about a universe made up of the same atoms as the brain cells that enable me to do the wondering.

I can also stare into the same star-filled night sky and see an indifferent, cold Cosmos. Rather than progressing to a better state, the Universe appears to be a monstrous, destructive, incomprehensible confection of black holes and warped time and space with little good to show for itself. What in God's name could have caused God in Genesis to affirm that He was pleased with what He saw or had accomplished? Yet out of this Cosmos has briefly come a creature that sweats, breathes, pees, has apelike hair and shape, who thrills to the sound of a Mozart concerto, exults at the sight of the Taj Majal, delights in reading a Wordsworth poem. It's odd, unreasonable, absurd. How to accommodate to such a Cosmos? Becker answers that you and I must recruit God or gods, our help in ages past.

The Nobel biologist E.O. Wilson agrees. The need to believe is genetically implanted in us, Wilson avers. "The brain is made for religion, and religion was made for the brain."

Since I'm genetically wired to believe in something, where is my faith best posited? In Christianity? Judaism? Atheism . . . definitely, there is no God at all? Faith in the law of Nature? Fly to the foothills of the Himalayas to be guided by the spiritual guru familiar to us in cartoons . . . the robed Eastern mystic perched on a cliff dispensing nuggets of wisdom? Take a week for a silent retreat, meditating. One out of every seven Americans now practices meditation of some kind, triple the number in 2012.

People into meditation and Eastern religion envisage that upon dying they may merge into pure awareness, becoming one with universal consciousness. The new appreciation of consciousness, as existing outside of ourselves, suggests that the survival of the individual essence, spirit, or soul is possible for all . . . formal religion not required.

In his 1925 work *The Everlasting Man*, the British writer and philosopher G.K. Chesterton criticized Eastern philosophies and religions, whose "argument includes everything, and in another sense comes to nothing. Their circularity is represented by a serpent with its tail in its mouth, or by the Swastika, where eternal life keeps changing from one point to another."

Chesterton belonged to the Oxford Movement that commenced in the nineteenth century with the conversion of prominent English Anglicans and agnostics to Roman Catholicism. I studied them in researching an article that I wrote for *Commonweal* and for *The Tablet* magazine about the conversion of the famous skier Sir Arnold Lunn, who became a significant apologist for Roman Catholicism beginning in 1933 (Chapter 18).

How, I ask myself, could brilliant, analytical minds like those of Lunn, Chesterton and Ronald Knox, Evelyn Waugh and Graham Greene and Malcolm Muggeridge, have become converts to a church ruled by prelates, many of whom turned out to be deplorable human beings? The only explanation I can find is that these brilliant men had explored every possible way to bear the burden of their existence, and turned their eyes toward Rome.

If you're not a believer, here's a question you might ask yourself, as I have: If the result of believing is to infuse your life with tranquility and happiness, why not believe? The seventeenth-century mathematician Blaise Pascal thought his wager was a good idea. It goes like this. The atheist, if he's right, has the satisfaction of knowing he's logically correct. But that's about all he gets. By contrast, the believer, whether he's right or wrong, gets to delight in the infinite divine happiness provided by a forgiving God, comprehended through Jesus Christ. Unfortunately, Pascal's famous wager, though comforting, is somewhat flawed. It's implausible to believe in something to make yourself happy when you're simultaneously aware that you contrived the belief. In his superb book *Sapiens*, about the evolution of our species, author Yuval Harari puts the matter more bluntly: happiness depends on self-delusion.

To live amid such delusion, uncertainty, and doubt demands a kind of cosmic heroism, believed Ernest Becker. We are enveloped in a mystery that will never be solved. The only way to get beyond the contradictions of our existence is not via popular psychotherapy, advised Becker, but to be healed in the timeworn religious way, by an all-embracing and all-justifying beyond . . . to project one's problems onto a god-figure.

"Be aware," wrote the Jesuit thinker Karl Rahner, "that for a long time He has been waiting for you in the deepest dungeon of your blocked-up heart."

THE AUTHOR

John Fry was the author of three books, the writer or editor of hundreds of published articles on skiing, travel, business, and religion, and the retired editorial director of a half-dozen outdoor magazines published by the New York Times Co. and Times Mirror Co.

Born in Montreal in 1930, Fry graduated from McGill University in 1951, majoring in philosophy and economics.

He emigrated in 1957 to New York City where he became managing editor of the daily newspaper *American Metal Market*. He toured northern Europe reporting on the four-year-old European Common Market organization in Brussels, and wrote numerous editorials on economics and politics for the newspaper.

Once a collegiate ski racer, he was named editor in chief of *Ski*, America's oldest and largest ski magazine, in 1964. He subsequently worked also as editorial director of *Golf* and *Outdoor Life* magazines, with circulations ranging from 350,000 to 1.8 million. He originated the National Standard Race (NASTAR), similar to par in golf. In 1967 he created the Nations Cup, a way annually to rank the national teams competing in the World Cup of alpine skiing. He has written about his adventures skiing in Russia, China, Africa's Atlas Mountains, the Andes, and the Alps, and helicopter skiing in British Columbia.

From 1984 to 1988 Fry worked independently as a consultant. He was an early user of computer word processing, enabling freelancers to operate from their homes. He wrote a column on editing for *Folio*, the magazine of magazine management. He worked on the startup of *European Travel & Life Magazine* and of *Golf Course Living*, and served as editorial consultant for Environmental Nutrition.

In 1988, the New York Times Sports/Leisure Group hired Fry to create a new magazine, *Snow Country*. It was named by the Acres of Diamonds Awards in 1991 as one of America's best new magazines. In 1996, he was named editor of New Magazine Development. In this role he started *Golf Course Living* magazine. He retired from the New York Times Co. in 1999. He lived in Katonah, N.Y., with his wife Marlies, and died two days after his 90th birthday in 2020.

A dedicated gardener, Fry designed a hillside garden at his passive solar home, displaying sculptures by his daughter, featured in the June 15, 2011 edition of *The New York Times*.

A director of the Pinchot Institute for Conservation, he helped to initiate two national conferences on the environmental impact of the rapid growth in mountain living. He also served as a director and the treasurer of Riverkeeper, a pioneer organization combating pollution on the Hudson River.

Books

A Mind at Sea, Henry Fry and the glorious era of Quebec-built giant sailing ships, Dundurn Press, Toronto, 2013.

The Story of Modern Skiing, University Press of New England, 2006.

No Hill Too Fast, with Phil and Steve Mahre, Simon & Schuster, New York, 1985. Biography of the Olympic and World Cup champions.

Boards of Directors

Chairman, International Skiing History Association (ISHA), 2014-2020.

President, ISHA, 2001–2004, 2011–2014.

Director, Pinchot Institute for Conservation, 1994–1999.

Director, Treasurer, Riverkeeper, 1992–2000.

Director, Beaver Dam Sanctuary, 1995–2020.

Articles published

More than 300 published articles and columns on skiing and travel.

"The Priest Won," *Commonweal magazine,* June 5, 2009.

"Up and Down the Holy Mountains," *The Tablet,* December 2009.

Awards

Elected to the U.S. National Ski Hall of Fame, one of only two people ever to solo into the Hall.

Lifetime Achievement Award of the International Skiing History Association.

Federation Internationale de Ski (FIS) Journalism Award, 1997.

U.S. Dept. of Agriculture Certificate of Appreciation for Exceptional Contribution to Rural Development, Washington, DC.

Addendum: 'John Fry journalist' at Wikipedia.

Media That Informed This Book

Texts that shaped and informed the author in writing *Abandon Foolish Scheme*:

Americanavalancheassociation.org—The Snowy Torrents.

Oxford Dictionary of Quotations. In it, citations for death, dead, and dying outnumber those for live, life and living.

The Gospel of John, with commentary by William Barclay, 1955.

Somewhere Towards the End, by Diana Athill.

The Kingdom—Story of the early Christians whose unlikely beliefs conquered the world, by Emmanuel Carrere, English translation, 2017.

The Adversary—A True Story of Monstrous Deception, by Emmanuel Carrere, 2002.

The Songlines—The invisible pathways of Australia's Aborigines, by Bruce Chatwin, 1987.

Orthodoxy, by G.K. Chesterton, 1908.

The Everlasting Man, by G.K. Chesterton, 1925.

A Sort of Life—Autobiography by Graham Greene, 1971.

Sapiens—A Brief History of Mankind, by Yuval Noah Harari, 2011.

God Is Not Great—How Religion Poisons Everything, by Christopher Hitchens, Audiobook 2007.

Scott & Amundsen—The Race to the South Pole, by Roland Huntford, 1979.

Psychedelic Prophets—The Letters of Aldous Huxley and Humphry Osmond, 2018.

The Varieties of Religious Experience, by William James, 1902.

Book of Job, Old Testament, oldest book in the Bible, 6th C. BCE.

When Breath Becomes Air, by Paul Kalanithi, 2016.

What Shall We Say?—Evil, Suffering, and the Crisis of Faith, by Thomas G. Long, 2011.

Captain Kidd and the War Against the Pirates, by Robert C. Ritchie, 1986.

Concluding Unscientific Postscript to the Philosophical Fragments —An Existential Contribution, by Soren Kierkegaard, 1846.

JFK'S Secret Doctor—The Remarkable Life of Medical Pioneer and Legendary Rock Climber Hans Kraus, by Susan E.B. Schwartz, 2012.

Biocentrism—How Life and Consciousness Are the Keys to Understanding the True Nature of the Universe, by Robert Lanza with Robert Berman, 2009.

The Intelligence of the Cosmos—New Answers from the Frontiers of Science, by Ervin Laszlo, 2017.

Mere Christianity, by C.S. Lewis, 1943.

Difficulties—Being a Correspondence about the Catholic Religion between Ronald Knox and Arnold Lunn, 1932.

Conjugal Love, by Alberto Moravia, 1949.

A Third Testament—A Modern Pilgrim Explores the Spiritual Wanderings of Augustine, Blake, Pascal, Tolstoy, Bonhoeffer, Kierkegaard, and Dostoevsky, by Malcolm Muggeridge, 1976.

Moral Man & Immoral Society—A Study in Ethics and Politics, by Reinhold Niebuhr, 1932.

The Concept of Mind, by Gilbert Ryle, 1949.

A Course in Miracles—Circle of Atonement, Based on the Original Handwritten Notes of Helen Schucman, Part 1, 1976.

The World's Religions, by Huston Smith, revised edition 2009.

The Modern Book of the Dead, by Ptolemy Tomkins, 2012.

Mysticism—The Nature and Development of Spiritual Consciousness, by Evelyn Underhill, 1993.

"The Age of Creativity," by Emily Urquhart—November 2017 article in Canada's *The Walrus* magazine.

My Bright Abyss—Meditation of a Modern Believer, by Christian Wiman, 2013.